At Sylvan, we believe reading is one of life's most important, most personal, most meaningful skills and we're so glad you've taken this step to become a successful reader with us. We know spelling, vocabulary, and reading comprehension are all critical to successful, thoughtful, and rewarding reading. A strong foundation in reading takes third-graders from learning to read to reading to learn, a new phase of learning and discovery to the world around you.

At Sylvan, successful reading instruction encompasses numerous reading processes with research-based, developmentally appropriate, and highly motivating, entertaining, and thought-provoking lessons. The learning process relies on high standards and meaningful parental involvement. With success, students feel increasing confidence. With increasing confidence, students build even more success. It's a perfect cycle. That's why our Sylvan workbooks aren't like the others. We're laying out the roadmap for learning. The rest is in your hands.

Parents, you have a special role. While your child is working, stay within earshot. If he needs help or gets stuck, you can be there to get him on the right track. And you're always there with supportive encouragement and plenty of celebratory congratulations.

One of the best ways to see learning progress is to check one's own work. Each section of the workbook includes a Check It! strip. As your child completes the activities, he can check his answers with Check It! If he sees any errors, he can fix them himself.

At Sylvan, our goal is confident readers who have the skills to tackle anything they want to read. We love learning. We want all children to love it as well.

We hope you and your child enjoy *Sylvan 3rd-Grade Super Reading Success*. As your child continues on his academic journey, your local Sylvan Learning Center can also partner with your family in ensuring your child remains a confident, successful, and independent learner! Turn the page for more information and a special offer on our in-center service.

The Sylvan Team

Sylvan Learning Center.
Unleash your child's potential here.

No matter how big or small the academic challenge, every child has the ability to learn. But sometimes children need help making it happen. Sylvan believes every child has the potential to do great things. And, we know better than anyone else how to tap into that academic potential so that a child's future really is full of possibilities. Sylvan Learning Center is the place where your child can build and master the learning skills needed to succeed and unlock the potential you know is there.

The proven, personalized approach of our in-center programs deliver unparalleled results that other supplemental education services simply can't match. Your child's achievements will be seen not only in test scores and report cards but outside the classroom as well. And when he starts achieving his full potential, everyone will know it. You will see a new level of confidence come through in everything he does and every interaction he has.

How can Sylvan's personalized in-center approach help your child unleash his potential?

• Starting with our exclusive Sylvan Skills Assessment®, we pinpoint your child's exact academic needs.

• Then we develop a customized learning plan designed to achieve your child's academic goals.

• Through our method of skill mastery, your child will not only learn and master every skill in his personalized plan, he will be truly motivated and inspired to achieve his full potential.

To get started, included with this Sylvan product purchase is $10 off our exclusive Sylvan Skills Assessment®. Simply use this coupon and contact your local Sylvan Learning Center to set up your appointment.

And to learn more about Sylvan and our innovative in-center programs, call 1-800-EDUCATE or visit www.educate.com. *With over 1,000 locations in North America, there is a Sylvan Learning Center near you!*

3rd-Grade
Super Reading Success

Copyright © 2009 by Sylvan Learning, Inc.

Published in the United States by Random House, Inc., New York, and in Canada by Random House of Canada Limited, Toronto.

www.tutoring.sylvanlearning.com

Created by Smarterville Productions LLC
Cover and Interior Photos: Jonathan Pozniak
Cover and Interior Illustrations: Duendes del Sur

First Edition

ISBN: 978-0-375-43006-0

Library of Congress Cataloging-in-Publication Data available upon request.

This book is available at special discounts for bulk purchases for sales promotions or premiums. For more information, write to Special Markets/Premium Sales, 1745 Broadway, MD 6-2, New York, New York 10019 or e-mail specialmarkets@randomhouse.com.

PRINTED IN CHINA

10 9 8 7 6

Spelling Contents

Vocabulary Contents

Reading Comprehension Contents

Checking your answers is part of the learning.

Each section of the workbook begins with an easy-to-use Check It! strip.

1. Before beginning the activities, cut out the Check It! strip.

2. As you complete the activities on each page, check your answers.

3. If you find an error, you can correct it yourself.

Compound Words

1

Keywords

A COMPOUND WORD is a word that's made up of two words stuck together, like *treehouse* or *skateboard* or *dogsled*.

READ the paragraph. The words in **bold** are your keywords.

When it's warm **outside**, I like to play in my **backyard** all day. I run in the grass **barefoot**, and I lie down in the br... **sunshine. Sometimes** I play **baseball** or **football** with friends. Today is my **birthday**, so we're having a party. M... **grandmother** gave us each a yummy **cupcake** and some ... **popcorn** to eat. My friends will stay until **sunset**, when it gets dark. We'll have a lot of fun, as long as it doesn't rain!

FILL IN the blanks with the **bold** words in alphabetical order.

1. _____   7. _____
2. _____   8. _____
3. _____   9. _____
4. _____   10. _____
5. _____   11. _____
6. _____   12. _____

✓ Check It!

Page 1

Keywords

1. backyard	7. grandmother
2. barefoot	8. outside
3. baseball	9. popcorn
4. birthday	10. sometimes
5. cupcake	11. sunset
6. football	12. sunshine

Page 2

Split It!

grandmother
↓
grand + mother

1. backyard	7. grandmother
2. barefoot	8. outside
3. baseball	9. popcorn
4. birthday	10. sometimes
5. cupcake	11. sunset
6. football	12. sunshine

Page 3

Blank Out!

	Bonus:
1. barefoot	1. backpack
2. backyard	2. campfire
3. birthday	3. airplane
4. baseball	4. bedtime
5. cupcake	5. handwriting
6. sunset	6. seasick
7. popcorn	
8. outside	

Page 4

Add It Up

1. bedroom	10. housework
2. blackboard	11. lighthouse
3. bookcase	12. peanut
4. carefree	13. playground
5. courtroom	14. shopveil
6. downstairs	15. silkworm
7. fireworks	16. snowstorm
8. footstep	17. zigzag
9. highway	

1

3rd-Grade Spelling Success

Keywords

A COMPOUND WORD is a word that's made up of two words stuck together, like *treehouse* or *skateboard* or *dogsled*.

READ the paragraph. The words in **bold** are your keywords.

When it's warm **outside**, I like to play in my **backyard** all day. I run in the grass **barefoot**, and I lie down in the bright **sunshine**. **Sometimes** I play **baseball** or **football** with friends. Today is my **birthday**, so we're having a party. My **grandmother** gave us each a yummy **cupcake** and some **popcorn** to eat. My friends will stay until **sunset**, when it gets dark. We'll have a lot of fun, as long as it doesn't rain!

FILL IN the blanks with the **bold** words in alphabetical order.

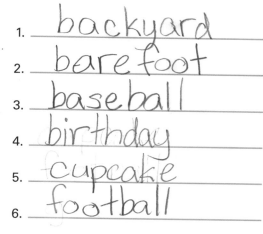

1. backyard
2. barefoot
3. baseball
4. birthday
5. cupcake
6. football
7. grandmother
8. outside
9. popcorn
10. sometimes
11. sunset
12. sunshine

Split It!

Which one of the keywords has more than two syllables?

grandmother

How many syllables does it have? __3__

Break it down: What two smaller words make up the bigger word?

grand + _mother_

When you split a compound word into syllables, start by breaking it down into the smaller words and putting a dot in between the words. Then, if one of the words has more than one syllable (like _mother_), put a dot between the syllables.

SPLIT the keywords into syllables, using dots to mark the breaks.

Examples: skate•board, step•fa•ther

backyard	1. back•yard
barefoot	2. bare•foot
baseball	3. base•ball
birthday	4. birth•day
cupcake	5. cup•cake
football	6. foot•ball
grandmother	7. grand•mother
outside	8. out•side
popcorn	9. pop•corn
sometimes	10. some•times
sunset	11. sun•set
sunshine	12. sun•shine

Blank Out!

FILL IN the blanks with keywords.

1. Without shoes or socks, your *foot* is *bare*.
   You are _barefoot_.

2. The grassy *yard* in the *back* of our house is the _backyard_.

3. Every year you celebrate the *day* of your *birth*. Happy _Birthday_!

4. If you hit a *ball* and run to a *base*, you're playing _baseball_.

5. A small *cake* shaped like a *cup* is a _cupcake_.

6. After the *sun* has *set*, it's dark outside. Be home by _sunset_!

7. If you heat up a kernel of *corn*, it will *pop*. That's called _popcorn_.

8. When you go *out* the front or back *side* of your house, you're _outside_.

Bonus

Can you finish these sentences?

1. A *pack* that you fill with books and carry on your *back* is a _backpack_.

2. When you *camp* in a tent and roast marshmallows over a *fire*,
   that's a _campfire_.

3. A *plane* that flies through the *air* from New York to London is an _airplane_.

4. At night, when the clock says it's *time* to go to *bed*, it's _bedtime_.

5. The words you are *writing* with your pen in your *hand* is _pencil_.

6. If sailing on the *sea* makes you so *sick* you
   throw up, you're _seasick_.

Compound Words

Add It Up

ADD UP the smaller words to make compound words.
SPLIT the new words into syllables. FILL IN the blanks, using dots to mark the breaks.

Example: skate + board = skate•board

bed	+ room	=	1.	bed•room
black	+ board	=	2.	black•board
book	+ case	=	3.	book•case
care	+ free	=	4.	care•free
court	+ room	=	5.	court•room
down	+ stairs	=	6.	down•stairs
fire	+ works	=	7.	fire•works
foot	+ step	=	8.	foot•step
high	+ way	=	9.	high•way
house	+ work	=	10.	house•work
light	+ house	=	11.	light•house
pea	+ nut	=	12.	pea•nut
play	+ ground	=	13.	play•ground
shop	+ lift	=	14.	shop•lift
silk	+ worm	=	15.	silk•worm
snow	+ storm	=	16.	snow•storm
zig	+ zag	=	17.	zig•zag

✓ Check It!

Cut out the Check It! section on page 1, and see if you got the answers right.

Keywords

Two-syllable words with a DOUBLE CONSONANT in the middle (like *middle*) are easy to split into syllables. The dot goes between the double letters, just like this: mid•dle.

READ the paragraph. The words in **bold** are your keywords.

After **soccer** practice last week, I was in a **hurry**. Mom would **worry** and **holler** at me if I got home late. It was a **rotten**, rainy day. I was cold and grumpy. In my rush, I almost fell over a **kitten** in a **shallow puddle**! I picked her up so I could **carry** her home. I dried her off and tied a **ribbon** around her neck. She fell asleep on my **pillow**. Now she will **follow** me everywhere!

FILL IN the blanks with the **bold** words in alphabetical order.

1. carry
2. follow
3. holler
4. hurry
5. kitten
6. pillow
7. puddle
8. ribbon
9. rotten
10. shallow
11. soccer
12. worry

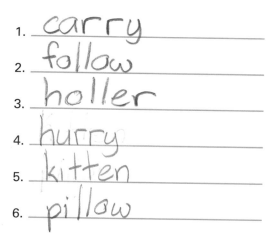

✓ Check It!

Page 5

Keywords

1. carry
2. follow
3. holler
4. hurry
5. kitten
6. pillow
7. puddle
8. ribbon
9. rotten
10. shallow
11. soccer
12. worry

Page 6

Split It!

1. car•ry
2. fol•low
3. hol•ler
4. hur•ry
5. kit•ten
6. pil•low
7. pud•dle
8. rib•bon
9. rot•ten
10. shal•low
11. soc•cer
12. wor•ry

Page 7

Blank Out!

1. kitten
2. carry
3. follow
4. hurry
5. worry
6. rotten
7. holler

Mix & Match

1. attack
2. banner
3. collect
4. current
5. million
6. possess
7. pollute
8. tunnel
9. yellow
10. scatter

Page 8

Spotlight

Consonants: b, c, d, f, g, h, j, k, l, m, n, p, q, r, s, t, v, w, x, y, z
Vowels: a, e, i, o, u (sometimes y)

Split It!

Double Consonants	Double Vowels
1. hobby	1. aardvark
2. lasso	2. creepy
3. merry	3. needle
4. sputter	4. scooper
5. upper	5. skiing

Split It!

SPLIT the keywords into syllables, using dots to mark the breaks.

HINT: Remember, the split happens between the double letters.

Example: middle   mid•dle

carry	1. car·ry
follow	2. fol·low
holler	3. hol·ler
hurry	4. hur·ry
kitten	5. kit·ten
pillow	6. pil·low
puddle	7. pud·dle
ribbon	8. rib·bon
rotten	9. rot·ten
shallow	10. shal·low
soccer	11. soc·cer
worry	12. wor·ry

Blank Out!

FILL IN the blanks with keywords.

HINT: The answer words rhyme with the italicized words.

1. I've just *written* the cutest story about a ___kitten___.

2. My dog, *Barry*, likes to ___carry___ his bone everywhere he goes.

3. Turn left by the *hollow* tree, then ___follow___ the path.

4. When Sonya's in a ___hurry___, she moves so fast, she's almost *blurry*.

5. Don't ___worry___ about Fido getting cold. He's really *furry*!

6. I've never *gotten* even a card from Aunt Jill. Isn't that ___rotten___?

7. My dad starts to ___hollow___ when he gets hot under the *collar*.

Mix & Match

In each box, MATCH a syllable on the left with a syllable on the right to make a word. DRAW a line between the two syllables to match them. REWRITE the words you matched in the blanks.

HINT: All the words have a double consonant in the middle.

at	rent
ban	lion
col	tack
cur	lect
mil	ner

1. ___attack___
2. ___banner___
3. ___collect___
4. ___current___
5. ___million___

pos	low
pol	ter
tun	lute
yel	nel
scat	sess

6. ___possess___
7. ___pollute___
8. ___tunnel___
9. ___yellow___
10. ___scatter___

Spotlight on Consonants and Vowels

You know the difference between a consonant and a vowel, right? Let's check your skills.

List all the consonants in the alphabet:

b,c,d,f,g,h,j,k,l,m,n,p,q,r,s,t,v,
w,x,y,z

List all the vowels in the alphabet:

a,e,i,o,u

Stack Up

SORT the words into the categories. PUT the words in each list in alphabetical order.

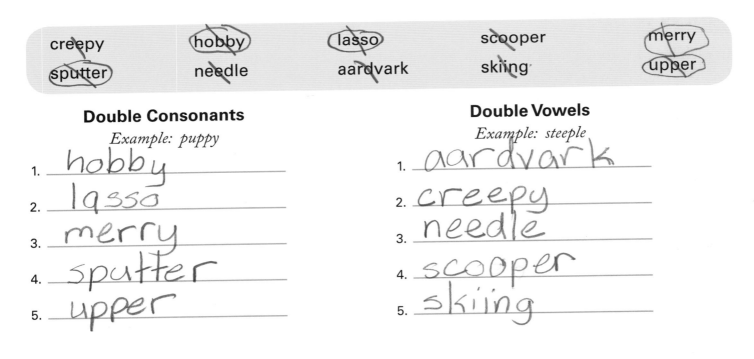

| creepy | hobby | lasso | scooper | merry |
| sputter | needle | aardvark | skiing | upper |

Double Consonants
Example: puppy

1. hobby
2. lasso
3. merry
4. sputter
5. upper

Double Vowels
Example: steeple

1. aardvark
2. creepy
3. needle
4. scooper
5. skiing

✓ Check It!

Cut out the Check It! section on page 5, and see if you got the answers right.

Keywords

When you spell a word, first break it into SYLLABLES. Usually each syllable has one vowel sound. That vowel sound is a good clue to how to spell the syllable.

READ the paragraph. The words in **bold** are your keywords.

Last **winter**, I went to see the circus. First, there was a **lady** acrobat wearing a pretty **costume** made of sparkly **fabric**. Then, the clowns ran out dressed like cowboys at a **rodeo**. One of them was riding a giant **chicken**! In the **final** act of the **program**, a magician covered an empty **basket** with a soft **velvet** scarf and then waved his wand. When he pulled the scarf away, there was a baby **tiger** inside! What a **super** show!

FILL IN the blanks with the **bold** words in alphabetical order.

1. basket
2. chicken
3. costom
4. fabric
5. final
6. lady
7. program
8. rodeo
9. super
10. tiger
11. velvet
12. winter

✓ Check It!

Page 9

Keywords

1. basket
2. chicken
3. costume
4. fabric
5. final
6. lady
7. program
8. rodeo
9. super
10. tiger
11. velvet
12. winter

Page 10

Stack Up

Long Vowel Sound	Short Vowel Sound
1. final	1. basket
2. lady	2. chicken
3. program	3. costume
4. rodeo	4. fabric
5. super	5. velvet
6. tiger	6. winter

Page 11

Split It!

1. bas•ket	7. pro•gram
2. chick•en	8. ro•de•o
3. cos•tume	9. su•per
4. fab•ric	10. ti•ger
5. fi•nal	11. vel•vet
6. la•dy	12. win•ter

Add It Up

1. mi•ser / mis•ter	4. du•ty / dust•y
2. ga•ble / gam•ble	5. fi•ber / fib•ber
3. su•per / sup•per	6. po•lar / pop•lar
	7. u•nit / un•fit

Page 12

Blank Out!

1. student	6. hotel
2. label	7. standards
3. honor	8. evil
4. vanish	9. vapors
5. exit	10. level

Pick the One!

1. ex|it (e|vil)	4. stan|dards
2. (ho|tel) hon|or	(stu|dent)
3. (la|bel) lev|el	5. (va|por) van|ish

Stack Up

You know that in the word *baker*, the vowel sound of the first syllable is a LONG **a**. A long **a** says its name. In the word *banker*, the first vowel sound is a SHORT **a**.

READ the keywords out loud. SORT them by the vowel sound in their first syllable.

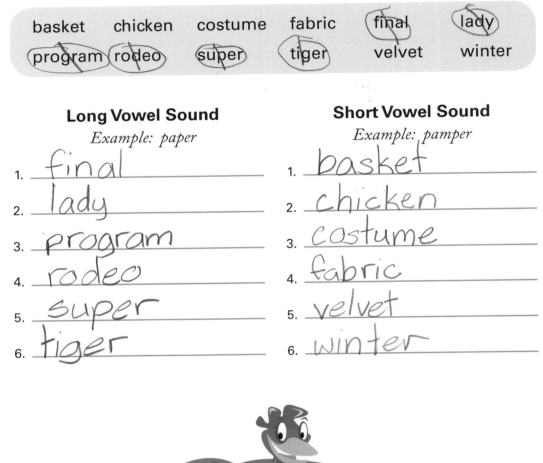

basket   chicken   costume   fabric   final   lady
program   rodeo   super   tiger   velvet   winter

Long Vowel Sound
Example: paper

1. final
2. lady
3. program
4. rodeo
5. super
6. tiger

Short Vowel Sound
Example: pamper

1. basket
2. chicken
3. costume
4. fabric
5. velvet
6. winter

Split It!

SPLIT the keywords into syllables, using dots to mark the breaks.

HINT: If the vowel is long, the syllable usually ends in a vowel. If the vowel is short, the syllable usually ends in a consonant.

Examples: fi•nal, fin•ish

basket	1. bas • ket	program	7. pro • gram
chicken	2. chick • en	rodeo	8. ro • de • o
costume	3. cos • tume	super	9. su • per
fabric	4. fab • ric	tiger	10. ti • ger
final	5. fa • nal	velvet	11. vel • vet
lady	6. la • dy	winter	12. win • ter

Add It Up

ADD the letters to the middle of the words to make new words. Then SPLIT the new words into syllables, using dots to mark the breaks.

Example: baker: ba•ker + n = ban•ker

1. miser + t = mi • ser / mis • ter
2. gable + m = ga • ble / gam • ble
3. super + p = su • per / sup • per
4. duty + s = du • ty / dus • ty
5. fiber + b = fi • ber / fib • ber
6. polar + p = po • lar / pop • lar
7. unit + f = un • it / un • fit

Blank Out!

FILL IN the blanks with the words.

evil	exit	hotel	honor	label
level	standards	student	vapors	vanish

1. Shanice does her homework, so she's a good _student_.

2. The _label_ on my shirt says "dry clean only."

3. We sang a song in _honor_ of soldiers who died in wars.

4. The hamster must be somewhere. He didn't just _vanish_!

5. If there's a fire, use the emergency _exit_.

6. Instead of camping, we stayed in a _hotel_.

7. Coach Patel is always talking about our team's high _standards_

8. Tonya may be bad, but she's not _evil_.

9. The factory gives off steam and other _vapors_.

10. Tory is already on _level_ 3 of the videogame.

Pick the One!

CIRCLE the word in each pair that starts with a syllable that has a long vowel. SPLIT both words into syllables by drawing a line to mark the break.

Example: (hu|man)   hum|ble

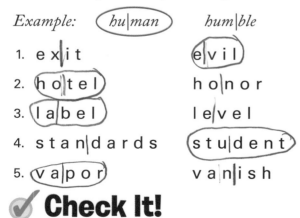

1. e x|i t   (e|v i l)
2. (h o|t e l)   h o|n o r
3. (l a|b e l)   l e|v e l
4. s t a n|d a r d s   (s t u|d e n t)
5. (v a|p o r)   v a n|i s h

✓ Check It!

Cut out the Check It! section on page 9, and see if you got the answers right.

Keywords

The word *oodles* means "a lot." There are oodles of words that end in a consonant + "-le" (like *noodle*, *bottle*, or *pickle*). We'll call them OODLES. In most oodles, the syllable split comes right before the consonant + "-le" (like jun•gle).

READ the paragraph. The words in **bold** are your keywords.

I read a good book with a **purple** cover. The **title** was *Life in 1865*. Imagine living in the **middle** of the 1800s. Instead of driving a car, you'd go to the **stable**, and put a **saddle** and a **bridle** on a horse and ride it. You might have a whole herd of **cattle** or just one cow for milk. You'd make your own clothes using a **needle** and thread, with a **thimble** to protect your finger. At night you'd have to put a **candle** on the dinner **table** for light. Could you **handle** all that?

FILL IN the blanks with the **bold** words in alphabetical order.

1. _____   7. _____

2. _____   8. _____

3. _____   9. _____

4. _____   10. _____

5. _____   11. _____

6. _____   12. _____

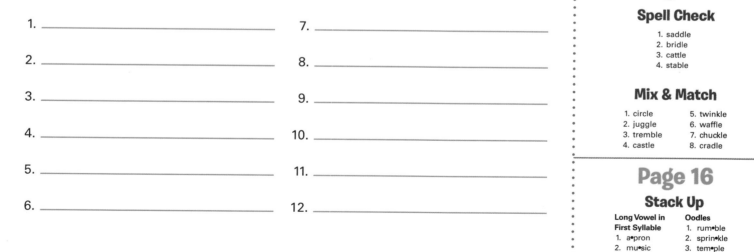

✓ **Check It!**

Page 13
Keywords

1. bridle
2. candle
3. cattle
4. handle
5. middle
6. needle
7. purple
8. saddle
9. stable
10. table
11. thimble
12. title

Page 14
Split It!

1. bri•dle
2. can•dle
3. cat•tle
4. han•dle
5. mid•dle
6. nee•dle
7. pur•ple
8. sad•dle
9. sta•ble
10. ta•ble
11. thim•ble
12. ti•tle

Page 15
Spell Check

1. saddle
2. bridle
3. cattle
4. stable

Mix & Match

1. circle
2. juggle
3. tremble
4. castle
5. twinkle
6. waffle
7. chuckle
8. cradle

Page 16
Stack Up

Long Vowel in First Syllable
1. a•pron
2. mu•sic
3. pro•duce
4. pri•vate

Oodles
1. rum•ble
2. sprin•kle
3. tem•ple
4. gen•tle

Double Consonants
1. pat•tern
2. con•nect
3. les•son
4. ban•ner

Split It!

Oodles follow all the rules you've already learned. SPLIT the keywords into syllables, using dots to mark the breaks.

Example: lit•tle   ca•ble   twin•kle

bridle	1. _____
candle	2. _____
cattle	3. _____
handle	4. _____
middle	5. _____
needle	6. _____
purple	7. _____
saddle	8. _____
stable	9. _____
table	10. _____
thimble	11. _____
title	12. _____

Spell Check

READ the ad. CIRCLE the four keywords that are misspelled.
FILL IN the blanks with those misspelled words. Spell them right!

Big Sale at Bubba's Horse Center!

Need a new sadel? We've got the best! How about a bridel? We've got that too!

We've even got cowboy gear for all you cattel ranchers! All our staybel items are

half-priced! We're not horsing around at Bubba's!

1. _____   3. _____

2. _____   4. _____

Mix & Match

MATCH a syllable on the left with a syllable on the right to make a word.
DRAW a line between the two syllables to match them. REWRITE the
words you matched in the blanks.

Example: an gle → angle

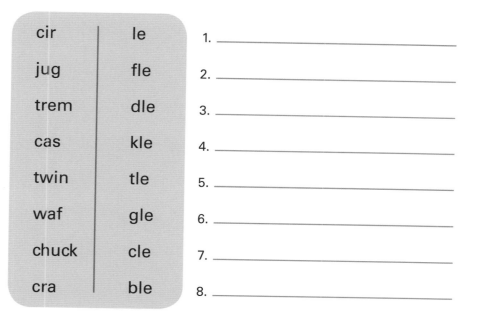

cir	le
jug	fle
trem	dle
cas	kle
twin	tle
waf	gle
chuck	cle
cra	ble

1. _____

2. _____

3. _____

4. _____

5. _____

6. _____

7. _____

8. _____

Stack Up

SORT the words into the categories. SPLIT the words into syllables, using dots to mark the breaks.

rumble	connect	apron	music	private	pattern
sprinkle	produce	lesson	temple	banner	gentle

Long Vowel in First Syllable
Example: bak•er

1. _____

2. _____

3. _____

4. _____

Oodles
Example: cir•cle

1. _____

2. _____

3. _____

4. _____

Double Consonants
Example: mid•dle

1. _____

2. _____

3. _____

4. _____

 **Check It!**

Cut out Check It! to see if you got the answers right.

Pick the One!

CIRCLE the correct syllable split in each pair.

Example: (jun•gle) jung•le

1. m e • t a l   m e t • a l
2. d r a • g o n   d r a g • o n
3. f i n • i s h   f i • n i s h
4. s e • c o n d   s e c • o n d
5. h o • n e s t   h o n • e s t
6. h u • m a n   h u m • a n
7. l e • v e l   l e v • e l
8. s t u • d e n t   s t u d • e n t

Add It Up

ADD UP the smaller words to make compound words. SPLIT the new words into syllables. FILL IN the blanks, using dots to mark the breaks.

Example: rattle + snake = rat•tle•snake

gentle	+ man	=	1.	_____
butter	+ milk	=	2.	_____
news	+ paper	=	3.	_____
pepper	+ mint	=	4.	_____
human	+ kind	=	5.	_____
sky	+ rocket	=	6.	_____
jelly	+ fish	=	7.	_____
motor	+ cycle	=	8.	_____

Grid Lock

Here's a list of compound words:

basketball	supermarket	butterfly	grandmother
grasshopper	afternoon	watermelon	fingertip
underground	ladybug		

FILL IN the grid with the compound words, writing one letter in each box starting from the left. Be sure to put each word in a row of the right length.

HINT: Pay close attention to where the syllable dots are in the row.

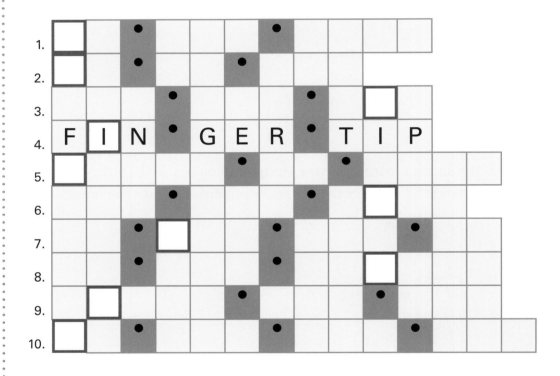

Bonus

The highlighted boxes spell the word for a bunch of large reptiles with snapping jaws. What's the word?

✓ Check It!

Cut out Check It! to see if you got the answers right.

Keywords

Any special ending that you add to a word to change its meaning (even a little) is called a SUFFIX.

A VERB is an action word, like *run* or *sit* or *yell*. Verbs have different suffixes depending on who is doing the action and when:

Verb	*yell*
Add "-s"	He yells.
Add "-ing"	I am yelling now.
Add "-ed"	I yelled yesterday.

READ the paragraph. The words in **bold** are your keywords.

I love a barbecue! Mom **greets** the guests and **boils** the corn while Dad **grills** the burgers. I always have to **remind** him to **melt** some cheese on mine! Our dog loves to **smell** the meat while it **cooks**. After dinner, the grownups **talk** and the little kids **scatter** all over the backyard to **play** games. Soon everyone is **screaming** for dessert. I **want** to eat barbecue every day!

FILL IN the blanks with the **bold** words in alphabetical order.

1. _____   7. _____

2. _____   8. _____

3. _____   9. _____

4. _____   10. _____

5. _____   11. _____

6. _____   12. _____

Bonus

CIRCLE the other verbs in the paragraph.

✓ Check It!

Page 19

Keywords

1. boils	7. remind
2. cooks	8. scatter
3. greets	9. screaming
4. grills	10. smell
5. melt	11. talk
6. play	12. want

Bonus: love, have, loves, is, eat

Page 20

Alternate Endings

+ "-s"	+ "-ing"	+ "-ed"
1. boils	boiling	boiled
2. cooks	cooking	cooked
3. greets	greeting	greeted
4. grills	grilling	grilled
5. melts	melting	melted
6. plays	playing	played
7. reminds	reminding	reminded
8. scatters	scattering	scattered
9. screams	screaming	screamed
10. smells	smelling	smelled
11. talks	talking	talked
12. wants	wanting	wanted

Page 21

Write It Right!

1. greeted	4. melted
2. boiled	5. reminded
3. scattered	6. smelled

Alternate Endings Again!

+ "-s"	+ "-ing"	+ "-ed"
1. attends	attending	attended
2. barks	barking	barked
3. collects	collecting	collected
4. knocks	knocking	knocked
5. groans	groaning	groaned
6. warns	warning	warned

Verbs, Verbing, Verbed

✓ Check It!

Page 22

Pick the One!

1. began
2. heard
3. saw
4. thought
5. bought
6. got
7. said
8. took
9. knew
10. did

Blank Out!

1. knew
2. began
3. thought
4. bought
5. heard

Alternate Endings

ADD the three endings to the keyword verbs.

Example: act   acts   acting   acted

Verb	Verb + "-s"	Verb + "-ing"	Verb + "-ed"
boil	1. _____	_____	_____
cook	2. _____	_____	_____
greet	3. _____	_____	_____
grill	4. _____	_____	_____
melt	5. _____	_____	_____
play	6. _____	_____	_____
remind	7. _____	_____	_____
scatter	8. _____	_____	_____
scream	9. _____	_____	_____
smell	10. _____	_____	_____
talk	11. _____	_____	_____
want	12. _____	_____	_____

Write It Right!

READ each sentence. UNSCRAMBLE the **bold** word. FILL IN the blanks with the unscrambled words. HINT: All of the words use the past tense "-ed" verb ending.

1. My teammates **tergede** me with a cheer as soon as I walked in.

2. Do you like hot dogs grilled or **delobi**?

3. The papers I dropped **testardec** in the wind.

4. The snowman **temdle** in the sun.

5. I'm glad you **merddine** me about the party tonight.

6. Clinton **lemsled** so bad after the game, we told him to hit the shower!

Alternate Endings Again!

ADD "-s," "-ing," and "-ed" to these verbs. FILL IN the blanks with the new words.

Example: start   starts   starting   started

Verb	Verb + "-s"	Verb + "-ing"	Verb + "-ed"
attend	1.		
bark	2.		
collect	3.		
knock	4.		
groan	5.		
warn	6.		

Verbs, Verbing, Verbed

Pick the One!

Instead of adding "-ed" to the end of a verb to make it happen in the past, sometimes you have to change the spelling of the whole verb. One example is *run*. The past tense of *run* is *ran*.

CIRCLE the correct past tense verb form of the word in the box.

Example: run   runned   (ran)   ranned

1.	begin	began	beginned	beganned
2.	hear	heard	heared	herded
3.	see	seed	sawed	saw
4.	think	thought	thinked	thoughted
5.	buy	buyed	bought	boughten
6.	get	gat	getted	got
7.	say	said	sayed	sed
8.	take	taked	toked	took
9.	know	knew	knowed	knewed
10.	do	doed	done	did

Blank Out!

FILL IN the blanks with oddball verbs.

1. I was sure that I _____ this guy, but I couldn't remember his name.

2. When the starter waved his flag, the race _____.

3. I _____ about the party all day before deciding not to go.

4. Stefan went to the store and _____ a new hat.

5. I'm not sure what I _____, but it sounded loud and scary.

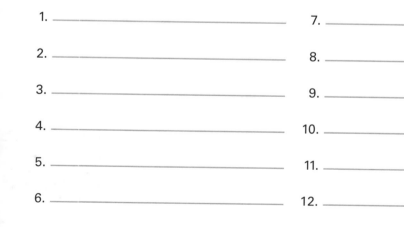

Keywords

To make words PLURAL (more than one), you usually just add an "-s." But when a word ends in "ch," "sh," "x," "o," or "ss," you usually add "-es" to make it plural. Adding "-es" often adds a syllable.

READ the paragraph. The words in **bold** are your keywords.

Dad and I take long **hikes** in the country. We set out early, carrying our **lunches**. We pass through **fields** and small towns with white **churches**. Sometimes we pick **bunches** of **flowers** to bring home to Mom. One time, we saw a pair of **foxes** standing **inches** away from us. I ask Dad a lot of **questions** about the things we see, and he always has good **answers**. He says we should all be **students** of nature. When we get back to the car, we treat ourselves like **heroes** and get a big pizza dinner. That's the best part of the day!

FILL IN the blanks with the **bold** words in alphabetical order.

1. _____

2. _____

3. _____

4. _____

5. _____

6. _____

7. _____

8. _____

9. _____

10. _____

11. _____

12. _____

✔ Check It!

Page 23

Keywords

1. answers
2. bunches
3. churches
4. fields
5. flowers
6. foxes
7. heroes
8. hikes
9. inches
10. lunches
11. questions
12. students

Page 24

Stack Up

"-s" Plurals	"-es" Plurals
1. an•swers	1. bunch•es
2. fields	2. church•es
3. flow•ers	3. fox•es
4. hikes	4. he•roes
5. ques•tions	5. inch•es
6. stu•dents	6. lunch•es

Page 25

Spell Check

1. bunches
2. inches
3. heroes
4. lunches
5. questions
6. flowers

Alternate Endings

1. beaches
2. blankets
3. chapters
4. flashes
5. fountains
6. guests
7. lobsters
8. masses
9. porches
10. potatoes
11. servants
12. successes

Page 26

Spotlight on More Verb Endings

1. matches
2. mixes
3. brushes
4. wishes
5. stitches
6. presses
7. confesses
8. reaches
9. attaches
10. relaxes
11. rushes
12. vanishes

Stack Up

READ the keywords out loud. SORT the keywords by their plural endings. SPLIT the words into syllables (if they have more than one), using dots to mark the breaks.

HINT: The syllable break *usually* comes before the "-es" plural ending.

Example: socks   dress•es

| answers | bunches | churches | fields | flowers | foxes |
| heroes | hikes | inches | lunches | questions | students |

"-s" Plurals	**"-es" Plurals**
1. _____	1. _____
2. _____	2. _____
3. _____	3. _____
4. _____	4. _____
5. _____	5. _____
6. _____	6. _____

Spell Check

READ the diary entry. CIRCLE the six keywords that are misspelled.
FILL IN the blanks with those misspelled words. Spell them right!

Dear Diary:

I messed up everything today! I made bunchiz of mistakes on my history test.
And I couldn't make centimeters into inchiz in math class. In English, we had to
talk about our heerose, and I didn't have any. When Stefanie and I were eating
our lunchiz, she kept asking me kwestionz about stuff I didn't know. Worst of all, I
forgot to get floworz for Mom's birthday. Am I a total doofus, or what?

1. _____   4. _____

2. _____   5. _____

3. _____   6. _____

Alternate Endings

ADD the "-s" or "-es" ending to these words to make them plural.

HINT: Remember, if the word ends in "ch," "sh," "x," "o," or "ss," it takes "-es."

Example: bug   bugs

Singular	Plural		Singular	Plural	
beach	1. _____		lobster	7. _____	
blanket	2. _____		mass	8. _____	
chapter	3. _____		porch	9. _____	
flash	4. _____		potato	10. _____	
fountain	5. _____		servant	11. _____	
guest	6. _____		success	12. _____	

Spotlight on More Verb Endings

The "-es" rule goes for verbs too. So when a verb ends in "ch," "sh," "x," "o," or "ss," you usually need to add "-es" to make it the right form. This usually adds a syllable. Try it out!

ADD "-es" to each verb.

Example: fix   fixes

Verb	Verb + "-es"
match	1. _____
mix	2. _____
brush	3. _____
wish	4. _____
stitch	5. _____
press	6. _____
confess	7. _____
reach	8. _____
attach	9. _____
relax	10. _____
rush	11. _____
vanish	12. _____

7

Keywords

When a word ends in "y," you have to drop the "y" and add "-ies" to make it a plural. This does not usually add a syllable. For example, *(lady – y) + ies = ladies*

READ the paragraph. The words in **bold** are your keywords.

My uncle owns two **companies** that make snowboards. He has **factories** in five different **countries** and offices in many big **cities**. More and more **families** are snowboarding nowadays. I've even seen a few **babies** learning how! People like nothing better than stretching their **bodies** to the limit, flying down a mountain under clear, blue **skies**. But many skiers who own **properties** in mountain **communities** complain that snowboarders are taking over their **territories** and refusing to share the slopes. They tell **stories** of accidents caused by rude behavior. Everyone needs to be careful.

FILL IN the blanks with the **bold** words in alphabetical order.

1. _____
2. _____
3. _____
4. _____
5. _____
6. _____
7. _____
8. _____
9. _____
10. _____
11. _____
12. _____

✓ Check It!

Page 27

Keywords

1. babies
2. bodies
3. cities
4. communities
5. companies
6. countries
7. factories
8. families
9. properties
10. skies
11. stories
12. territories

Page 28

Alternate Endings

1. baby
2. body
3. city
4. community
5. company
6. country
7. factory
8. family
9. property
10. sky
11. story
12. territory

Page 29

Write It Right!

1. factories
2. stories
3. properties
4. communities
5. countries
6. companies

Bonus: copies

Alternate Endings

1. blueberries
2. bunnies
3. butterflies
4. centuries
5. colonies
6. copies
7. diaries
8. libraries
9. memories
10. mysteries
11. pennies
12. societies

✅ Check It!

Page 30

**Spotlight on Verbs
That End in "Y"**

+ "-s"	+ "-ing"	+ "-ed"
1. buries	burying	buried
2. carries	carrying	carried
3. dries	drying	dried
4. fries	frying	fried
5. empties	emptying	emptied
6. hurries	hurrying	hurried
7. marries	marrying	married
8. tries	trying	tried
9. worries	worrying	worried

Alternate Endings

FILL IN the blanks with the singular forms of the keywords.

Example: ladies   lady

Plural	Singular
babies	1. _____
bodies	2. _____
cities	3. _____
communities	4. _____
companies	5. _____
countries	6. _____
factories	7. _____
families	8. _____
properties	9. _____
skies	10. _____
stories	11. _____
territories	12. _____

Write It Right!

UNSCRAMBLE the keywords. HINT: They all end in "-ies."

1. My family has visitied all the jellybean **seftocari** in California.

_ _ ☐ _ _ _ _ _ _ _

2. My grandpa tells lots of great **irestos** about my parents.

_ _ ☐ _ _ _ _

3. The people around here don't like when I walk my dog on their **tippeesorr**.

☐ _ _ _ _ _ _ _ _

4. Many **usimminocet** have a neighborhood watch program.

_ _ _ _ _ _ ☐ _ _ _

5. Someday, I want to travel to lots of foreign **stirounce**.

_ _ _ _ _ _ _ ☐ _

6. My parents both work for computer **pomnicesa**.

_ _ _ _ _ _ _ _ ☐ _

Bonus: The boxed letters spell twins, triplets, or clones!

☐ ☐ ☐ ☐ ☐ ☐

Alternate Endings

DROP the "y" and ADD an "-ies" to each word to make it plural. WRITE the new words.

Singular	Plural	Singular	Plural
blueberry	1. _____	diary	7. _____
bunny	2. _____	library	8. _____
butterfly	3. _____	memory	9. _____
century	4. _____	mystery	10. _____
colony	5. _____	penny	11. _____
copy	6. _____	society	12. _____

Spotlight on Verbs That End in "Y"

Just like nouns that end in "y," when a verb ends in "y" (like *cry*), you have to drop the "y" and add "-ies" or "-ied" to get the right form. Be careful: You leave the "y" when you add "-ing."

FILL IN the blanks with the correct verb forms.

Example: cry   cries   crying   cried

Verb	Verb + "-s"	Verb + "-ing"	Verb + "-ed"
bury	1. _____	_____	_____
carry	2. _____	_____	_____
dry	3. _____	_____	_____
fry	4. _____	_____	_____
empty	5. _____	_____	_____
hurry	6. _____	_____	_____
marry	7. _____	_____	_____
try	8. _____	_____	_____
worry	9. _____	_____	_____

Keywords

Here are two more rules about plural suffixes:

Rule 1: If a word ends in an "f," then you have to drop the "f" and add "-ves" to make it plural. This usually does not add a syllable.

$$So: (calf - f) + ves = calves$$

$$Or: (knife - fe) + ves = knives$$

Rule 2: Some words have weird plurals, like *foot* and *feet*.

READ the paragraph. The words in **bold** are your keywords.

In the old days, farm families lived very busy **lives**. They took care of their animals, including the **calves**, **geese**, and **oxen**. They groomed their horses and checked their **teeth** and **hooves**. Dogs guarded against **wolves**. Cats kept **mice** out of the grain. While the **men** tended the fields, their **wives** made everything from **loaves** of bread to butter. Even the **children** had jobs to do!

FILL IN the blanks with the **bold** words in alphabetical order.

1. _____
2. _____
3. _____
4. _____
5. _____
6. _____
7. _____
8. _____
9. _____
10. _____
11. _____
12. _____

Stack Up

READ the keywords out loud. SORT the keywords by how they become plural. Then FILL IN the blanks with the singular forms of the words.

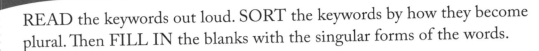

calves   children   geese   hooves   lives   loaves
men   mice   oxen   teeth   wives   wolves

"-f" to "-ves" Plurals
Example: knives   knife

Plural	Singular
1.	
2.	
3.	
4.	
5.	
6.	

Oddball Plurals
Example: feet   foot

Plural	Singular
1.	
2.	
3.	
4.	
5.	
6.	

Criss Cross

FILL IN the grid by answering the clues with keywords.

ACROSS

2. More than one man

4. More than one child

5. More than one tooth

DOWN

1. More than one ox

2. More than one mouse

3. More than one goose

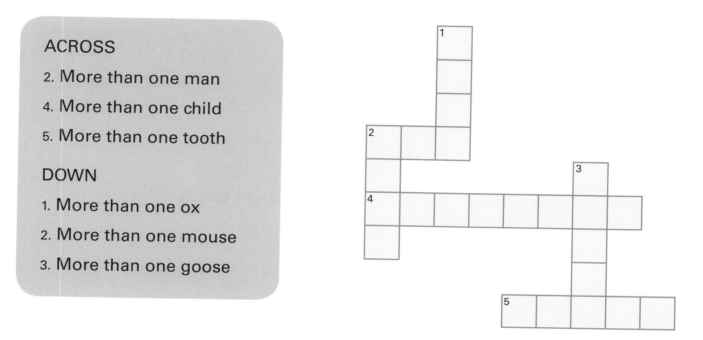

Alternate Endings

DROP the "f" or "fe" and ADD a "-ves" to these words to make them plural.
FILL IN the blanks with the plural words.

Example: life   lives

Singular	Plural	Singular	Plural
dwarf	1. _____	scarf	5. _____
half	2. _____	self	6. _____
knife	3. _____	shelf	7. _____
leaf	4. _____	thief	8. _____

Spotlight on Syllables

READ these plural words out loud. SORT the words by how many syllables they have. SPLIT the words into syllables, using dots to mark the breaks.

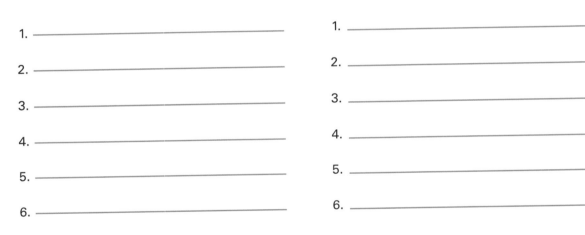

ditches	bushes	scarves	oxen	branches	knives
dice	moves	flies	hooves	boxes	inches

Example: slots   spac•es

One-Syllable Words

1. _____

2. _____

3. _____

4. _____

5. _____

6. _____

Two-Syllable Words

1. _____

2. _____

3. _____

4. _____

5. _____

6. _____

Word Search

FILL IN the blanks with the plural versions of the words listed. Then CIRCLE these plural words in the word grid. Words go down and across, not diagonally or backwards.

Example: lady   ladies

Singular		**Plural**
pillow	1.	_____
cherry	2.	_____
switch	3.	_____
torch	4.	_____
goose	5.	_____
thief	6.	_____
shelf	7.	_____
mouse	8.	_____
lasso	9.	_____
penny	10.	_____

```
R   V   S   W   I   T   C   H   E   S   L
O   T   H   I   E   V   E   S   G   Z   A
S   X   E   T   O   R   C   H   E   S   S
P   I   L   L   O   W   S   P   E   M   S
Q   W   V  (L   A   D   I   E   S)  I   O
C   H   E   R   R   I   E   S   E   C   E
M   Y   S   U   P   E   N   N   I   E   S
```

✓ Check It!

Page 35

Word Search

```
R V S W I T C H E S L
O T H I E V E S G Z A
S X E T O R C H E S S
P I L L O W S P E M S
Q W V L A D I E S I O
C H E R R I E S E C E
M Y S U P E N N I E S
```

Page 36

Split It!

1. news•pa•pers
2. grand•chil•dren
3. su•per•he•roes
4. prin•cess•es
5. lunch•box•es
6. bat•tle•ships
7. earth•quakes
8. house•wives

Alternate Endings

+ "-s"	+ "-ing"	+ "-ed"
1. empties	emptying	emptied
2. searches	searching	searched
3. approaches	approaching	approached
4. buries	burying	buried
5. displays	displaying	displayed
6. establishes	establishing	established

Split It!

SPLIT the compound words into syllables, using dots to mark the breaks.

newspapers	1. _____	
grandchildren	2. _____	
superheroes	3. _____	
princesses	4. _____	
lunchboxes	5. _____	
battleships	6. _____	
earthquakes	7. _____	
housewives	8. _____	

Alternate Endings

ADD the suffixes to the verbs listed.

Example: yell   yells   yelling   yelled

Verb	Verb + "-s"	Verb + "-ing"	Verb + "-ed"
empty	1. _____	_____	_____
search	2. _____	_____	_____
approach	3. _____	_____	_____
bury	4. _____	_____	_____
display	5. _____	_____	_____
establish	6. _____	_____	_____

Keywords

Adjectives are words that describe things, like *cool*. To say that ferrets are *cooler* than dogs, we make *cool* into a COMPARATIVE by adding the suffix "-er." To say llamas are the *coolest* pets of all, we make *cool* into a SUPERLATIVE by adding the suffix "-est."

READ the paragraph. The words in **bold** are your keywords.

In my family, Trisha is the **oldest**. She thinks she's **smarter** than everyone. My sister Ann is the **quietest** and **neatest** person ever! Derek is the **youngest**, but he's **taller** than I am. Mom says I'm the **wildest** one, and she wishes I were **calmer** and **cleaner**, like Ann. In sports, Dad can throw **longer**, but Derek is **quicker**, and I'm **stronger**. We have a lot of fun together.

FILL IN the blanks with the **bold** words in alphabetical order.

1. _____
2. _____
3. _____
4. _____
5. _____
6. _____
7. _____
8. _____
9. _____
10. _____
11. _____
12. _____

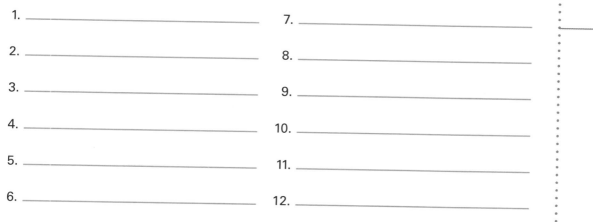

✓ **Check It!**

Page 37

Keywords

1. calmer
2. cleaner
3. longer
4. neatest
5. oldest
6. quicker
7. quietest
8. smarter
9. stronger
10. taller
11. wildest
12. youngest

Page 38

Alternate Endings

Comparative	Superlative
1. calmer	calmest
2. cleaner	cleanest
3. longer	longest
4. neater	neatest
5. older	oldest
6. quicker	quickest
7. quieter	quietest
8. smarter	smartest
9. stronger	strongest
10. taller	tallest
11. wilder	wildest
12. younger	youngest

Page 39

Word Blocks

1. calmer
2. wilder
3. quickest
4. neatest
5. younger
6. cleanest

Alternate Endings Again!

Comparative	Superlative
1. brighter	brightest
2. cheaper	cheapest
3. higher	highest
4. smoother	smoothest
5. weaker	weakest
6. blinder	blindest

Cool, Cooler, Coolest

✓ Check It!

Page 40

Spotlight on Something Fishy

1. tricky
2. brainy
3. gloomy
4. moody
5. satiny
6. silky
7. stumpy
8. smelly
9. wealthy
10. worthy
11. sweaty
12. shadowy

Bonus:

1. wrinkly
2. wiry
3. spongy
4. nobly
5. slimy

Alternate Endings

ADD the comparative and superlative suffix to each of the words.

Example: cool   cooler   coolest

Word	Comparative	Superlative
calm	1. _____	_____
clean	2. _____	_____
long	3. _____	_____
neat	4. _____	_____
old	5. _____	_____
quick	6. _____	_____
quiet	7. _____	_____
smart	8. _____	_____
strong	9. _____	_____
tall	10. _____	_____
wild	11. _____	_____
young	12. _____	_____

Word Blocks

One way to remember the spelling of a word is to picture its shape. Word blocks are a good way to practice.

Example: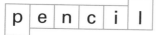

FILL IN the word blocks with words of the same shape from the list.

HINT: Look for double consonants and watch out for the word endings.

calmer   neatest   cleanest   younger   quickest   wilder

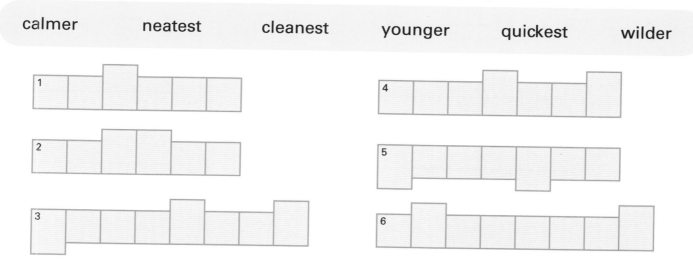

Alternate Endings Again!

ADD the suffixes to make the words into comparatives and superlatives.

Example: round   rounder   roundest

Word	Comparative	Superlative
bright	1. _____	_____
cheap	2. _____	_____
high	3. _____	_____
smooth	4. _____	_____
weak	5. _____	_____
blind	6. _____	_____

Spotlight on Something "Fish-y"

Suffixes can make a singular into a plural or an adjective into a superlative. You can also use suffixes to transform an ordinary noun, like *fish*, into an adjective just by adding "-y" to the end: *fishy*.

ADD "-y" to these nouns to make them into adjectives.

Example: fish fishy

Noun	Adjective		Noun	Adjective
trick	1. _____		stump	7. _____
brain	2. _____		smell	8. _____
gloom	3. _____		wealth	9. _____
mood	4. _____		worth	10. _____
satin	5. _____		sweat	11. _____
silk	6. _____		shadow	12. _____

Bonus

When a word ends in "e," you usually drop the "e" before adding the "-y."

Example: scale scaly

Noun	Adjective
wrinkle	1. _____
wire	2. _____
sponge	3. _____
noble	4. _____
slime	5. _____

Keywords

When a verb ends in a single vowel followed by a single consonant (like *tag*), you usually have to double the consonant before you add the verb endings "-ed" and "-ing." For example, *tag*, *tagged*, *tagging*.

READ the paragraph. The words in **bold** are your keywords.

Tonight I **starred** in the school play! I played a girl who was **planning** to leave home until her mother **begged** her to stay. At first I was **gripped** with fear and kept **skipping** lines. Then I **ripped** my costume, but we **pinned** it up backstage. Between acts I **grabbed** some food and water. I was afraid the show had **flopped**, but everyone **clapped** like crazy. Afterward people kept **stopping** by and **hugging** me. It was a success!

FILL IN the blanks with the **bold** words in alphabetical order.

1. _____
2. _____
3. _____
4. _____
5. _____
6. _____
7. _____
8. _____
9. _____
10. _____
11. _____
12. _____

✓ Check It!

Page 41

Keywords

1. begged
2. clapped
3. flopped
4. grabbed
5. gripped
6. hugging
7. pinned
8. planning
9. ripped
10. skipping
11. starred
12. stopping

Page 42

Alternate Endings

+ "s"	+ "-ing"	+ "-ed"
1. begs	begging	begged
2. claps	clapping	clapped
3. flops	flopping	flopped
4. grabs	grabbing	grabbed
5. grips	gripping	gripped
6. hugs	hugging	hugged
7. pins	pinning	pinned
8. plans	planning	planned
9. rips	ripping	ripped
10. skips	skipping	skipped
11. stars	starring	starred
12. stops	stopping	stopped

Page 43

Spell Check

1. skipped	3. grabbed
2. clapped	4. hugged

Stack Up

One-Syllable Words	Two-Syllable Words
1. begged	1. clap•ping
2. flopped	2. grab•bing
3. gripped	3. hug•ging
4. pinned	4. plan•ning
5. ripped	5. skip•ping
6. stopped	6. star•ring

Alternate Endings

ADD the suffixes to make each verb form.

HINT: You'll have to double the final consonant of each verb.

Example: tag   tags   tagging   tagged

Verb		Verb + "s"	Verb + "-ing"	Verb + "-ed"
beg	1.	_____	_____	_____
clap	2.	_____	_____	_____
flop	3.	_____	_____	_____
grab	4.	_____	_____	_____
grip	5.	_____	_____	_____
hug	6.	_____	_____	_____
pin	7.	_____	_____	_____
plan	8.	_____	_____	_____
rip	9.	_____	_____	_____
skip	10.	_____	_____	_____
star	11.	_____	_____	_____
stop	12.	_____	_____	_____

Spell Check

READ the diary entry. CIRCLE the four words that are misspelled. Then FILL IN the blanks with those misspelled words. Spell them right!

Dear Diary:

Today, Shanice and I skiped to the bus stop and sang a song to all the kids. Everyone claped along. Then, Shanice grabed Michael's hat, and we tossed it around. When we got on the bus, Shanice huged me and told me I was her best friend!

1. _____   3. _____

2. _____   4. _____

Stack Up

READ the words out loud. SORT them by how many syllables they have. FILL IN the blanks with the sorted words. SPLIT the words into syllables, using dots to mark the breaks.

HINT: Remember the double consonants!

| begged | clapping | flopped | grabbing | gripped | hugging |
| pinned | planning | ripped | skipping | starring | stopped |

One-Syllable Words
Example: clipped

1. _____

2. _____

3. _____

4. _____

5. _____

6. _____

Two-Syllable Words
Example: clip•ping

1. _____

2. _____

3. _____

4. _____

5. _____

6. _____

Spotlight on Comparatives and Superlatives

When a word ends in a single vowel and a single consonant, you have to double the consonant before you add "-er" or "-est" to make it a comparative or superlative. For example, *big, bigger, biggest*.

ADD the endings to make the words into comparatives and superlatives. WRITE the new words in the blanks next to the original word.

Example: big   bigger   biggest

Word	Comparative	Superlative
wet	1. _____	_____
fat	2. _____	_____
fit	3. _____	_____
hot	4. _____	_____
mad	5. _____	_____
red	6. _____	_____
sad	7. _____	_____
slim	8. _____	_____
tan	9. _____	_____
thin	10. _____	_____

Keywords

When an adjective ends in "e," you have to drop the last "e" before adding "-er" or "-est" to make it a comparative or superlative. For example, (*cute* – e) + er = *cuter*.

READ the paragraph. The words in **bold** are your keywords.

The Amazon Jungle used to be one of the **widest** forests in the world with the **purest** water. It is home to some of the **largest** animals, as well as the **strangest**. One of the **nicer**, **gentler** creatures is the sloth. It lives a **simple** life, eating the **finest** leaves and the **ripest** fruits. The sloth is **happiest** when it's asleep. Sadly, every year the sloth's **safe** world gets **closer** to being destroyed.

FILL IN the blanks with the **bold** words in alphabetical order.

1. _____

2. _____

3. _____

4. _____

5. _____

6. _____

7. _____

8. _____

9. _____

10. _____

11. _____

12. _____

✓ Check It!

Page 45
Keywords

1. closer
2. finest
3. gentler
4. happiest
5. largest
6. nicer
7. purest
8. ripest
9. safe
10. simple
11. strangest
12. widest

Page 46
Alternate Endings

Comparative	Superlative
1. closer	closest
2. finer	finest
3. gentler	gentlest
4. happier	happiest
5. larger	largest
6. nicer	nicest
7. purer	purest
8. riper	ripest
9. safer	safest
10. simpler	simplest
11. stranger	strangest
12. wider	widest

Page 47
Spotlight on Adjectives That End in "Y"

Comparative	Superlative
1. emptier	emptiest
2. fancier	fanciest
3. easier	easiest
4. merrier	merriest
5. trickier	trickiest
6. brainier	brainiest
7. gloomier	gloomiest
8. smellier	smelliest
9. wealthier	wealthiest
10. worthier	worthiest
11. scarier	scariest
12. sweatier	sweatiest

✓ Check It!

Page 48

Spotlight on Verbs That End in "E"

+ "-s"	+ "-ing"	+ "-ed"
1. bounces	bouncing	bounced
2. chases	chasing	chased
3. fades	fading	faded
4. hates	hating	hated
5. hopes	hoping	hoped
6. skates	skating	skated
7. smiles	smiling	smiled
8. stares	staring	stared
9. trades	trading	traded
10. trembles	trembling	trembled
11. wages	waging	waged
12. wiggles	wiggling	wiggled

Alternate Endings

ADD the suffixes to the words to make them comparatives and superlatives.

Example: tame   tamer   tamest

Word	Comparative	Superlative
close	1. _____	_____
fine	2. _____	_____
gentle	3. _____	_____
happy	4. _____	_____
large	5. _____	_____
nice	6. _____	_____
pure	7. _____	_____
ripe	8. _____	_____
safe	9. _____	_____
simple	10. _____	_____
strange	11. _____	_____
wide	12. _____	_____

Spotlight on Adjectives That End in "Y"

Remember our magic suffix that made nouns into adjectives? Well, it's *trickier* making adjectives into comparatives and superlatives. To make *happy* into a comparative or superlative, you have to drop the "y" and replace it with an "i." Go for it!

ADD the suffixes to make the words into comparatives and superlatives.

Example: happy   happier   happiest

Word	Comparative	Superlative
empty	1. _____	_____
fancy	2. _____	_____
easy	3. _____	_____
merry	4. _____	_____
tricky	5. _____	_____
brainy	6. _____	_____
gloomy	7. _____	_____
smelly	8. _____	_____
wealthy	9. _____	_____
worthy	10. _____	_____
scary	11. _____	_____
sweaty	12. _____	_____

Spotlight on Verbs That End in "E"

Just like with adjectives, when a verb ends in the letter "e," you have to drop the "e" before adding the "-ed" or "-ing" endings. For example, *like, liking, liked.*

FILL IN the blanks with the correct verb forms.

Example: wipe wipes wiping wiped

Verb		Verb + "-s"	Verb + "-ing"	Verb + "-ed"
bounce	1.	bounces	bouncing	bounced
chase	2.	chases	chasing	chased
fade	3.			
hate	4.			
hope	5.			
skate	6.			
smile	7.			
stare	8.			
trade	9.			
tremble	10.			
wage	11.			
wiggle	12.			

Word Blocks

FILL IN the word blocks with words of the same shape from the list.

HINT: Look for double consonants and watch out for the word endings.

| skipped | brighter | giggling | scariest | thinnest |
| switches | heroes | sprinkle | jungle | halfway |

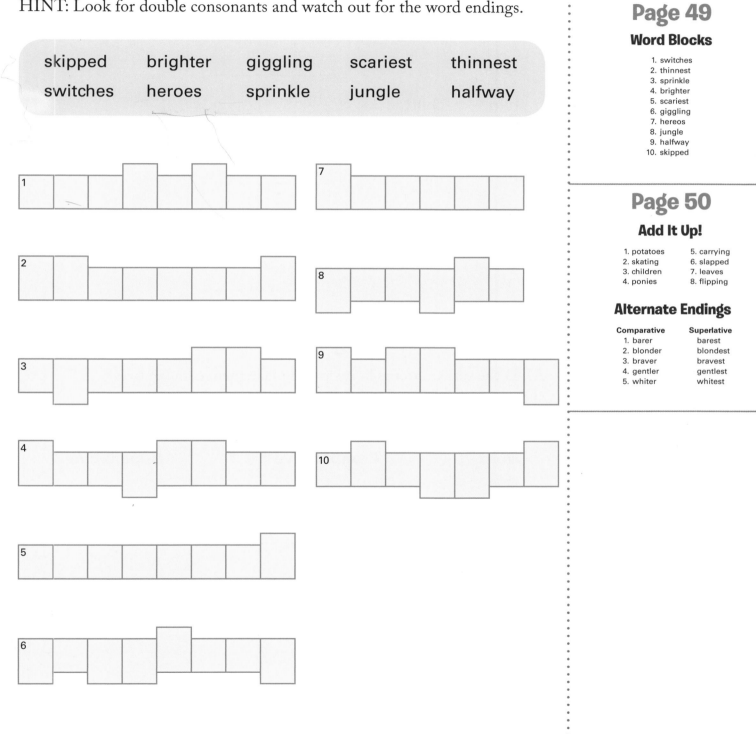

✓ Check It!

Page 49

Word Blocks

1. switches
2. thinnest
3. sprinkle
4. brighter
5. scariest
6. giggling
7. hereos
8. jungle
9. halfway
10. skipped

Page 50

Add It Up!

1. potatoes	5. carrying
2. skating	6. slapped
3. children	7. leaves
4. ponies	8. flipping

Alternate Endings

Comparative	Superlative
1. barer	barest
2. blonder	blondest
3. braver	bravest
4. gentler	gentlest
5. whiter	whitest

Add It Up

SOLVE the "problems" by adding the correct suffix.

Example: wolf + wolf = wolves

potato	+	potato	=	1. _____
skate	+	ing	=	2. _____
child	+	child	=	3. _____
pony	+	pony	=	4. _____
carry	+	ing	=	5. _____
slap	+	ed	=	6. _____
leaf	+	leaf	=	7. _____
flip	+	ing	=	8. _____

Alternate Endings

ADD the suffixes to the keywords to make them comparatives and superlatives.

Example: cute   cuter   cutest

Word	Comparative	Superlative
bare	1. _____	_____
blonde	2. _____	_____
brave	3. _____	_____
gentle	4. _____	_____
white	5. _____	_____

Keywords

Remember adjectives like *smooth* that describe things? Well, words that describe verbs are called ADVERBS. To make an adverb, just add the suffix "-ly" to the end of an adjective.

READ the paragraph. The words in **bold** are your keywords.

I was **totally** excited about Carla's costume party and **closely** watched the clock at school all day. The minutes ticked by so **slowly**. When I **finally** got home, I changed **rapidly** into my zombie costume. It fit **perfectly**. Everyone on the street looked at me **strangely**. I zipped **quickly** and **happily** to Carla's, where we stayed **mainly** in her backyard. **Sadly**, it started to rain, which **completely** ruined everything. Sigh.

FILL IN the blanks with the **bold** words in alphabetical order.

1. _____
2. _____
3. _____
4. _____
5. _____
6. _____

7. _____
8. _____
9. _____
10. _____
11. _____
12. _____

Split It!

SPLIT the keywords into syllables, using dots to mark the breaks.

HINT: The suffix "-ly" is always its own syllable.

Examples: smooth•ly

closely	1. _____
completely	2. _____
finally	3. _____
happily	4. _____
mainly	5. _____
quickly	6. _____
perfectly	7. _____
rapidly	8. _____
sadly	9. _____
slowly	10. _____
strangely	11. _____
totally	12. _____

Spell Check

READ Alicia's e-mail. CIRCLE the five keywords that are misspelled. FILL IN the blanks with those misspelled words. Spell them right!

> TO: Missy
>
> FROM: Alicia
>
> RE: Cheerleader Tryouts—Finaly!
>
> I totaly can't believe you missed tryouts today! Sharon was acting strangeley. She didn't say hi to me when I got there and was manely hanging out with Tye. I kwickilly put a stop to that by asking her what was wrong. She said she thought I didn't want her to make the team. I kompleatly cleared that up and we're friends again!

1. _____   4. _____

2. _____   5. _____

3. _____   6. _____

Alternate Endings

The keywords include the word *happily*. Did you notice that it's not *happyly*? Whenever an adjective ends in a "y," you have to replace the "y" with an "i" before making it an adverb. Try it.

TRANSFORM these adjectives into adverbs.

Example: sporty   sportily

Adjective	Adverb	Adjective	Adverb
angry	1. _____	pretty	5. _____
crazy	2. _____	lazy	6. _____
easy	3. _____	thirsty	7. _____
hungry	4. _____	speedy	8. _____

Spotlight on Making People Out of Verbs

Suffixes can turn nouns into adjectives (*sun* → *sunny*), adjectives into superlatives (*sunny* → *sunniest*), and adjectives into adverbs (*sunny* → *sunnily*). But did you know that the suffix "-er" can turn a verb into a noun?

FILL IN the blanks by adding the suffix "-er" to make the **bold** verb into a person.

HINT: Add "-er" to the basic verb form (remove the "-s").

*Example: A person who **works** is a **worker**.*

1. Manny **plays** football, so he's a football __player__.

2. If you **shop**, then you're a __shoper__.

3. A person who **teaches** is a __teacher__.

4. Kyle's dad **trains** athletes. He's a __trainer__.

5. If you **perform** on stage, then you're a __performer__.

6. Someone who **dances** is a __dancer__.

7. Mr. Santos loves to **golf**. He's a __golfer__.

8. If you **groom** dogs, you're a dog __groomer__.

9. A person who **walks** dogs is a dog __walker__.

10. Roberta **explores** the jungle. She's an __explorer__.

11. Something that **sharpens** pencils is a __sharpener__.

12. You use a __scraper__ to **scrape** the ice from your car.

Keywords

Here are three more suffixes for you to enjoy:

"-Ful" means *full of*, so *useful* means *full of use*.

"-Less" means *lacking*, so *useless* means *has no use*.

"-Ness" changes an adjective into a noun. For example: *happy → happiness*.

READ the paragraph. The words in **bold** are your keywords.

My band, Firecracker, was very **grateful** for the chance to play at this year's town fair. It was **wonderful**! We played a **handful** of songs under a **cloudless** sky in the main arena. Our lead singer, Robbie, got over her **shyness** about being on stage and became **fearless**! Then, one of the stage crew was **careless** and pulled out a wire. So we played the rest of the show in **darkness**. The **joyful** crowd loved it and the applause was **plentiful**. The mayor called us "**delightful**." Overall, our first concert was very **successful**!

FILL IN the blanks with the **bold** words in alphabetical order.

1. _____

2. _____

3. _____

4. _____

5. _____

6. _____

7. _____

8. _____

9. _____

10. _____

11. _____

12. _____

✓ Check It!

Page 55
Keywords

1. careless
2. cloudless
3. darkness
4. delightful
5. fearless
6. grateful
7. handful
8. joyful
9. plentiful
10. shyness
11. successful
12. wonderful

Page 56
Split It!

1. care•less
2. cloud•less
3. dark•ness
4. de•light•ful
5. fear•less
6. grate•ful
7. hand•ful
8. joy•ful
9. plen•ti•ful
10 shy•ness
11. suc•cess•ful
12. won•der•ful

Page 57
Spell Check

1. delightful   4. cloudless
2. wonderful   5. careless
3. fearless

Morph It!

1. careless   6. graceless
2. pitiless   7. helpful
3. fearless   8. doubtless
4. joyful   9. harmful
5. tasteful   10. faithless

Page 58
Spotlight on Piling on the Suffixes

1. skill•ful•ly   5. thank•ful•ly
2. care•less•ness   6. thought•less•ly
3. pain•less•ly   7. youth•ful•ness
4. hope•ful•ness

Alternate Endings

1. thoughtfulness 5. goodness
2. politeness   6. spotless
3. kindness   7. sweetness
4. homeless   8. spineless

Split It!

SPLIT the keywords into syllables, using dots to mark the breaks.

HINT: A suffix is usually its own syllable.

Example: use•ful

careless	1. _____
cloudless	2. _____
darkness	3. _____
delightful	4. _____
fearless	5. _____
grateful	6. _____
handful	7. _____
joyful	8. _____
plentiful	9. _____
shyness	10. _____
successful	11. _____
wonderful	12. _____

Spell Check

READ Carrie's thank-you note. CIRCLE the five keywords that are misspelled.
FILL IN the blanks with those misspelled words. Spell them right!

Hi Penny.

I had a (delitefull) time swimming in your (wunderfull) pool. You are so (feerliss) in the deep end! I'm glad the day was (clowdiless) By the way, I left my swimsuit in your bedroom. No wonder Mom calls me "(Careliss) Carrie!" I'll get it next weekend.

Carrie

1. delightful
2. wounderful
3. fearless

4. cloudless
5. Careless

Morph It!

Since "-less" is the opposite of "-ful," then *useless* is the opposite of *useful*. REPLACE "-less" or
"-ful" to make the opposite word. WRITE the opposite word on the blank.

Example: useful   useless

careful	1. _____	graceful	6. _____
pitiful	2. _____	helpless	7. _____
fearful	3. _____	doubtful	8. _____
joyless	4. _____	harmless	9. _____
tasteless	5. _____	faithful	10. _____

Spotlight on Piling on the Suffixes

Suffixes are like potato chips—you can't stop after just one! SPLIT these words into syllables, using dots to mark the breaks.

HINT: Suffixes are usually their own syllable, and each word has more than one suffix.

Example: usefulness   use•ful•ness

skillfully	1. _____
carelessness	2. _____
painlessly	3. _____
hopefulness	4. _____
thankfully	5. _____
thoughtlessly	6. _____
youthfulness	7. _____

Alternate Endings

When you add "-less" or "-ful" to a noun, it becomes an adjective. When you add "-ness" to an adjective, it becomes a noun.

ADD "-less" to the nouns to make them adjectives. ADD "-ness" to the adjectives to make them nouns. WRITE the new words on the blanks.

Example: shy   shyness   *Example: cloud   cloudless*

thoughtful	1. thoughtfulness	good	5. goodness
polite	2. politeness	spot	6. spotness
kind	3. kindness	sweet	7. sweetness
home	4. homeness	spine	8. spineness

Keywords

You sure know your suffixes! Here are some PREFIXES to try out:

"Pre-" means *before*, so *prepay* means *to pay beforehand*.
"Re-" means *again*, so *reheat* means *to heat again*.
"Mis-" means *wrong*, so a *mismatch* is *a wrong match*.
"Un-" means *not*, so *unfair* means *not fair*.

READ the paragraph. The words in **bold** are your keywords.

When you live by a river, flooding is not **uncommon** or **unexpected**. When I was in **preschool**, we were **unlucky**. We took every **precaution**. We had to **rebuild** and **repaint** our house after a big storm. Then, when I was a **preteen**, our basement flooded. I love our river, and it's hard to remember how it can **misbehave** during the rainy season. Its usual calm, flat surface is **misleading**. A lot of new neighbors were **misinformed** about flooding in this area, and they didn't **review** the information available. Boy, were they surprised!

FILL IN the blanks with the **bold** words in alphabetical order.

1. _____   7. _____

2. _____   8. _____

3. _____   9. _____

4. _____   10. _____

5. _____   11. _____

6. _____   12. _____

✓ Check It!

Page 59

Keywords

1. misbehave
2. misinformed
3. misleading
4. precaution
5. preschool
6. preteen
7. rebuild
8. repaint
9. review
10. uncommon
11. unexpected
12. unlucky

Page 60

Criss Cross

Across
1. unexpected
2. rebuild
3. misbehave
4. misleading

Down
1. uncommon
2. repaint

Page 61

Spell Check

1. precaution   3. misinformed
2. review   4. unlucky

Split It!

1. mis•be•have   7. re•build
2. mis•in•formed 8. re•paint
3. mis•lead•ing   9. re•view
4. pre•teen   10. un•com•mon
5. pre•cau•tion   11. un•ex•pect•ed
6. pre•school   12. un•luck•y

Page 62

Blank Out!

1. precook   6. prehistoric
2. rearrange   7. reinvent
3. misspell   8. misplace
4. unbuttoned   9. unfamiliar
5. pregame   10. mistreat

Bonus:
1. subway
2. subzero
3. subhuman

Criss Cross

FILL IN the grid by answering the clues with keywords.

ACROSS

1. Not expected

2. Build again

3. Behave wrongly

4. Leading the wrong way

DOWN

1. Not common

2. Paint again

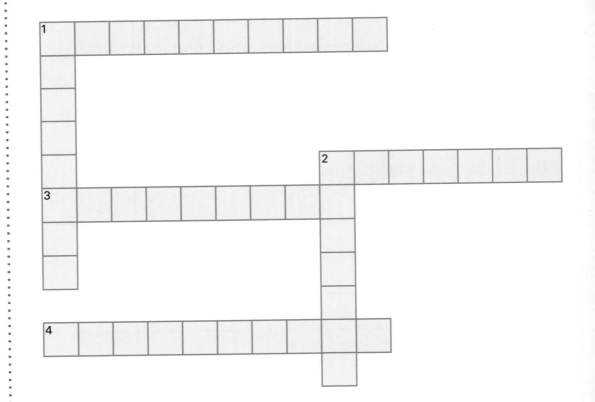

Spell Check

READ the diary entry. CIRCLE the four keywords that are misspelled.
FILL IN the blanks with those misspelled words. Spell them right!

> Dear Diary:
>
> My sister failed her driving test again! She took every (preekaushun)
> too. I even helped her to (riview) all the rules and signals. But she was
> missinformed about the time of the test, so she was late and nervous.
> Then she ran a red light! She is so unnlucky.

1. _____   3. _____

2. ~~Feteire~~ reView   4. _____

Split It!

SPLIT the keywords into syllables, using dots to mark the breaks.

HINT: A prefix is usually one syllable.

Example: predawn, pre•dawn

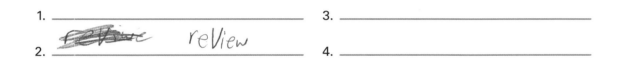

misbehave	1. mis•behave	rebuild	7. re•build
misinformed	2. mis•inform	repaint	8. re•paint
misleading	3. mis•leading	review	9. re•View
preteen	4. pre•teen	uncommon	10. un•common
precaution	5. pre•caution	unexpected	11. un•expcted
preschool	6. pre•school	unlucky	12. un•lucky

Blank Out!

ADD the prefix "pre-," "re-," "mis-," or "un-" to match the definitions. FILL IN the blanks with the new words.

Example: **re**use   *means to use again.*

1. _____cook means to cook beforehand

2. _____arrange means to arrange again.

3. _____spell means to spell wrong.

4. _____buttoned means not buttoned.

5. _____game means before the game.

6. _____historic means before recorded history.

7. _____invent means to invent again.

8. _____place means to put in the wrong place.

9. _____familiar means not familiar.

10. _____treat means to treat badly.

Bonus

The prefix "sub-" means *under* or *less than*.

ADD the prefix "sub-" to match the definition.

1. A _____way train goes under the ground.

2. _____zero temperatures are less than zero degrees.

3. Something _____human is less than human.

Criss Cross

FILL IN the grid by answering the clues with keywords.

HINT: You'll want to add a prefix or suffix to a word in the clue.

ACROSS

2. The most strange
3. Someone who drives
7. Under the soil
9. Fill again
10. To exist before
11. The wrong match

DOWN

1. Full of fear
4. Full of help
5. Read wrong
6. Lacking power
8. More brave than

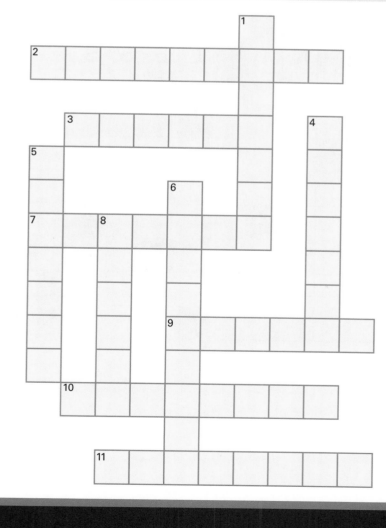

Grid Lock

FILL IN the grid with these words, writing one letter in each box starting from the left. Be sure to put each word in a row of the right length.

screwdriver	preteen	sharpener
wealthiest	unkindness	repossessing
subnormal	troublemaker	thoughtfulness
penniless	respectful	

HINT: Pay close attention to where the syllable dots are in the row.

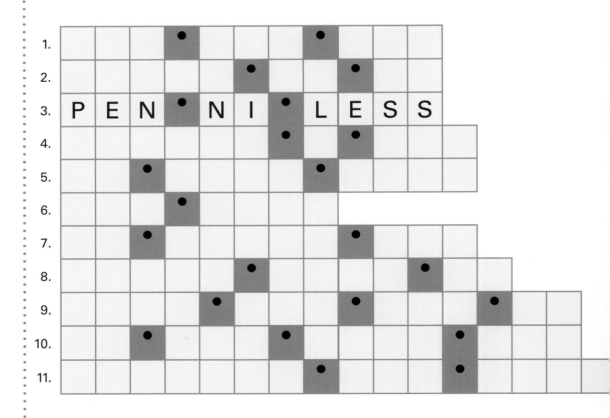

Keywords

When the letter "a" says its name, that's the long **a** sound, as in *hey* or *play* or *cake*. But hey! The word *hey* doesn't even have the letter "a" in it! Yep. The long **a** sound can be spelled lots of different ways.

READ the paragraph. The words in **bold** are your keywords.

During the winter **holiday**, my family went on a **sleigh** ride. There were **eight** of us, including our **neighbors**. We must have **weighed** a ton, but the horses flew **straight** down the **trail**, **spraying** snow with their hooves. They only needed a short **break** each hour. After the ride, we went out for a **steak** dinner. What a **great** day. I can't **wait** to do it again.

FILL IN the blanks with the **bold** words in alphabetical order.

1. _____

2. _____

3. _____

4. _____

5. _____

6. _____

7. _____

8. _____

9. _____

10. _____

11. _____

12. _____

Stack Up

READ the keywords out loud. SORT them by how the long **a** sound is spelled.

break ✓   eight ✓   great ✓   holiday ✓
neighbors ✓   sleigh ✓   spraying ✓   steak ✓
straight ✓   trail ✓   wait ✓   weighed ✓

Long A, Spelled "AY"
Example: play

1. ~~Play~~ holiday
2. Spraying

Long A, Spelled "EA"
Example: wear

1. Break
2. ~~Eat~~ Great
3. ~~Eat~~ neighbors

Long A, Spelled "AI"
Example: sail

1. trall
2. wait
3. Steak

Long A, Spelled "EIGH"
Example: neigh

1. eight
2. Straight
3. weighed
4. Sleigh

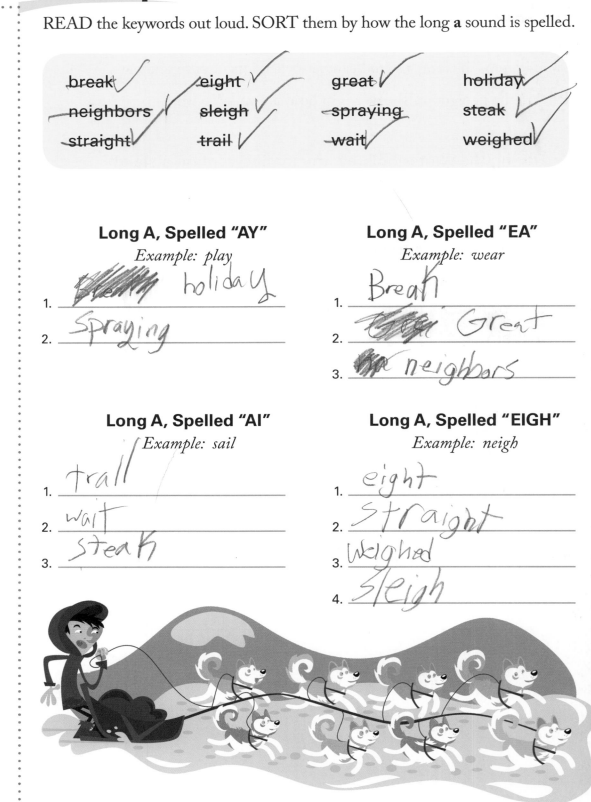

Blank Out!

FILL IN the blanks with keywords.

1. The band marched in a _Straight_ line.

2. Our next-door ~~~~ neighbors are moving away.

3. Uncle Troy wishes he _____ less.

4. Kyle built a computer when he was _____ years old.

5. Rare _____ is too gross to eat. Make mine well done!

6. Nick and I had a water fight while _____ the lawn. I won.

Write It Right!

FILL IN the missing letters to make the long **a** sound in each word.

Example: pl _a_ _y_

1. Don't be afr _a_ _i_ d.

2. I need a red cr _a_ _y_ on.

3. You shouldn't talk to str _a_ ngers.

4. Ask the teachers. Th _e_ _y_ should know.

5. Are you aw _a_ ke?

6. The sky is gr _a_ _y_ tod _a_ _y_.

7. A dog must ob _e_ _y_ its owner.

Grid Lock

Remember, no matter how many letters it takes to make a vowel sound, they usually stick together in one syllable, unless the double vowels come from a prefix, like in *preexist* or *reexamine*.

FILL IN the grid with these words, writing one letter in each box starting from the left. Be sure to put each word in a row of the right length.

| breakdown | reappear | campaign | neighborly |
| skyrocket | straighter | located | prearrange |

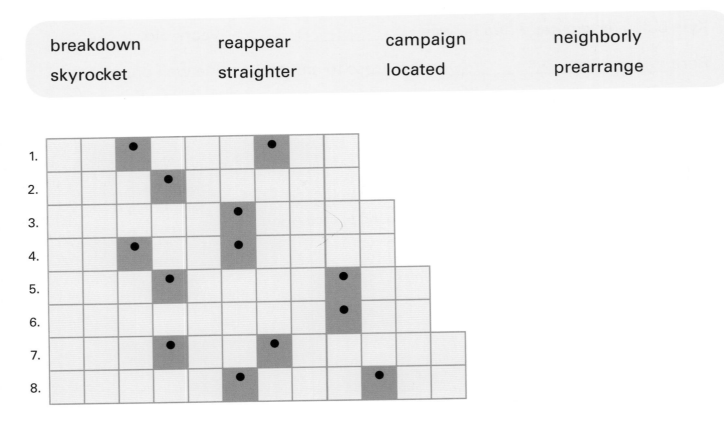

16

Keywords

There's more than meets the "i" in words like *high* and *dry*!
READ the paragraph. The words in **bold** are your keywords.

I was too **polite** to **deny** Great Aunt Ruby when she **invited** me to stay. Luckily one night seemed to **satisfy** her. She led me to the room I was to **occupy overnight**. The **firelight** made the shadows **multiply** into dozens of moving creatures. Suddenly I thought I saw a **slight** figure shimmering at my bedside! I began to sing a **lullaby**, then a nursery **rhyme** to calm myself down. When I turned on the light, there was nothing there. What a **fright**!

FILL IN the blanks with the **bold** words in alphabetical order.

1. _____
2. _____
3. _____
4. _____
5. _____
6. _____
7. _____
8. _____
9. _____
10. _____
11. _____
12. _____

✓ Check It!

Page 69

Keywords

1. deny
2. firelight
3. fright
4. invited
5. lullaby
6. multiply
7. occupy
8. overnight
9. polite
10. rhyme
11. satisfy
12. slight

Page 70

Stack Up

Long I Spelled "I-consonant-E"
1. invited
2. polite

Long I Spelled "IGH"
1. firelight
2. fright
3. overnight
4. slight

Long I Spelled "Y"
1. deny
2. lullaby
3. multiply
4. occupy
5. rhyme
6. satisfy

Page 71

Criss Cross

Across
2. rhyme
4. lullaby
5. satisfy
6. occupy

Down
1. deny
3. multiply

Spell Check

1. airtight
2. might
3. delighted
4. fright
5. slight
6. eyesight

Page 72

Grid Lock

1. hair • style
2. im • po • lite
3. de • ny
4. mag • ni • fy
5. mul • ti • ply
6. oc • cu • py
7. in • vit • ed
8. po • lite

Bonus:

+ "ed"	+ "ing"
1. magnified	magnifying
2. multiplied	multiplying
3. satisfied	satisfying
4. terrified	terrifying

Stack Up

READ the keywords out loud. SORT them by how the long **i** sound is spelled.

deny	firelight	fright	invited
lullaby	multiply	occupy	overnight
polite	rhyme	satisfy	slight

Long I, Spelled "I-consonant-E"
Example: kite

1. _____

2. _____

Long I, Spelled "Y"
Example: try

1. _____

2. _____

3. _____

4. _____

5. _____

6. _____

Long I, Spelled "IGH"
Example: tight

1. _____

2. _____

3. _____

4. _____

Criss Cross

FILL IN the grid by answering the clues with keywords.

ACROSS

2. A pair of words that sound alike

4. A sleepy song

5. Fulfill or please

6. Take up space, live in

DOWN

1. Turn down or refuse

3. Make more (like 6 x 2)

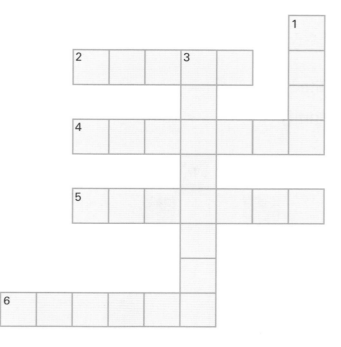

Spell Check

READ each sentence. CIRCLE the word that is misspelled. FILL IN the blanks with those misspelled words. Spell them right!

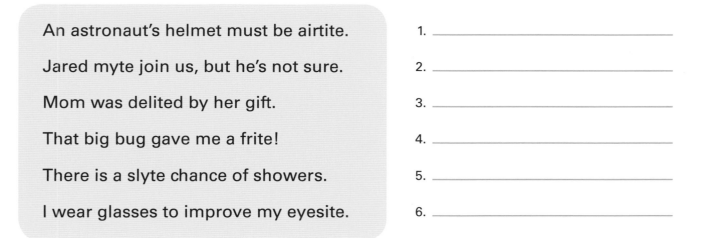

An astronaut's helmet must be airtite.

1. _____

Jared myte join us, but he's not sure.

2. _____

Mom was delited by her gift.

3. _____

That big bug gave me a frite!

4. _____

There is a slyte chance of showers.

5. _____

I wear glasses to improve my eyesite.

6. _____

Grid Lock

FILL IN the grid with these long **i** words, writing one letter in each box starting from the left. Be sure the dots properly break the words into syllables.

HINT: "-fy" is a suffix, so it's a separate syllable.

polite	occupy	invited	multiply
magnify	deny	hairstyle	impolite

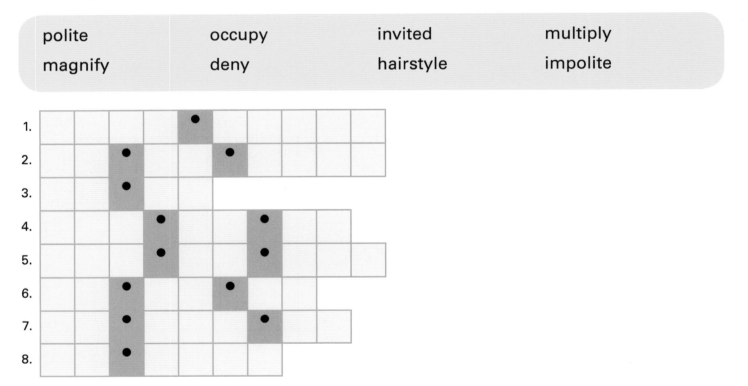

Bonus

ADD the verb endings to these verbs:

Example: cry, cried, crying

Verb	Verb + "-ed"	Verb + "-ing"
magnify	1. _____	_____
multiply	2. _____	_____
satisfy	3. _____	_____
terrify	4. _____	_____

Keywords

Long **u** sounds like **oo**, but it's not always spelled that way.

READ the paragraph. The words in **bold** are your keywords.

I'm in a weird mood. At breakfast, I couldn't **choose** between **grapefruit** or orange **juice**. This **afternoon**, I **threw** my homework in the sink by accident. I went to the mall with a **coupon** for shoes. It was a good **value**: ten dollars off. I met a **group** of friends from school. I had no **clue** they'd be there. We went to the food court and **moved** all the chairs to one side. I came home two hours late with shampoo instead of new shoes. Mom didn't **approve**. She says I have a **screw** loose!

FILL IN the blanks with the **bold** words in alphabetical order.

1. _____
2. _____
3. _____
4. _____
5. _____
6. _____

7. _____
8. _____
9. _____
10. _____
11. _____
12. _____

Bonus

CIRCLE the other words in the paragraph that have a long **u** sound.

✓ Check It!

Page 73

Keywords

1. afternoon
2. approve
3. choose
4. clue
5. coupon
6. grapefruit
7. group
8. juice
9. moved
10. screw
11. threw
12. value

Bonus:
mood, shoes, school, food, two, shampoo, shoes, loose

Page 74

Stack Up

Long U Spelled "OO"
1. afternoon
2. choose

Long U Spelled "OU"
1. coupon
2. group

Long U Spelled "UE"
1. clue
2. value

Long U Spelled "EW"
1. screw
2. threw

Long U Spelled "UI"
1. grapefruit
2. juice

Long U Spelled "O"
1. approve
2. moved

Page 75

Word Search

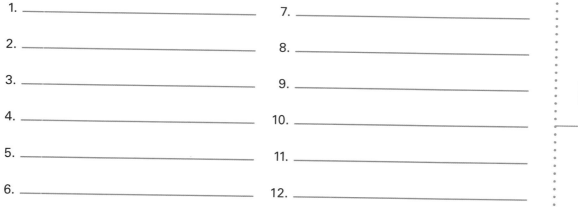

Page 76

Spotlight on "Yoo-hoo!"

1. educate
2. abuse
3. argue
4. fume
5. human
6. misuse
7. usual
8. beautiful
9. continue
10. avenue
11. fuel
12. monument
13. porcupine
14. refuse

Stack Up

READ the keywords out loud. SORT them by how the long **u** sound is spelled.

afternoon	approve	choose ✓	clue ✓
coupon	grapefruit	group	juice ✓
moved	screw	threw	value

Long U, Spelled "OO"
Example: soon

1. threw
2. ~~~~ juice

Long U, Spelled "OU"
Example: soup

1. clue
2. choose

Long U, Spelled "UE"
Example: due

1. _____
2. _____

Long U, Spelled "EW"
Example: chew

1. _____
2. _____

Long U, Spelled "UI"
Example: suit

1. _____
2. _____

Long U, Spelled "O"
Example: prove

1. _____
2. _____

Word Search

Oo-la-la! REWRITE the misspelled words, using the correct vowel(s) instead of "oo."
CIRCLE the words in the word grid. Words go down and across, not diagonally or backwards.

Example: noo, new

s**oo**per	1. _____
fr**oo**t	2. _____
st**oo**dent	3. _____
cr**oo**	4. _____
tr**oo**	5. _____
st**oo**	6. _____
bl**oo**berry	7. _____
sh**oo**maker	8. _____
y**oo**th	9. _____
n**oo**spaper	10. _____

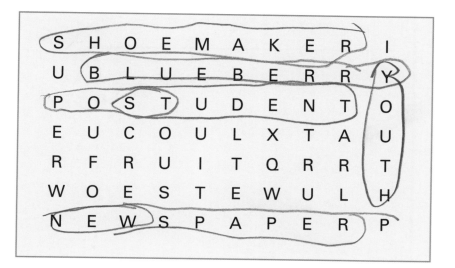

Spotlight on "Yoo-hoo!"

When the letter "u" says its name, it's usually spelled with a "u." REWRITE the words, replacing "yoo" with "u" to spell the word right.

HINT: Watch carefully for the "e" at the end of some words.

ed**yoo**cate	1. _____
ab**yoo**se	2. _____
arg**yoo**e	3. _____
f**yoo**me	4. _____
h**yoo**man	5. _____
mis**yoo**se	6. _____
yoos**yoo**al	7. _____
bea**yoo**tiful	8. _____
contin**yoo**e	9. _____
aven**yoo**e	10. _____
f**yoo**el	11. _____
mon**yoo**ment	12. _____
porc**yoo**pine	13. _____
ref**yoo**se	14. _____

Keywords

"E" is a really popular vowel. It gets lots of help from its friends. At the end of a word, the long **e** sound is usually made by "y" or "ey," like in *happy* and *donkey*. Inside a word, "e" gets help from "a" and "i" too, like in *neat* and *chief*.

READ the paragraph. The words in **bold** are your keywords.

Now that I'm a **teenager**, I have the weirdest dreams. They're a real **mystery** to me. **Actually**, the other night, I dreamed that a **monkey**, a **turkey**, and a **weasel** were hiding in my **chimney**. These **creatures** were **thieves**, coming to steal the plants out of our **greenhouse**. In my sleep, I didn't have the **energy** to stop them. My knees were weak, and I couldn't speak. Finally, I woke up. Can you **believe** it?

FILL IN the blanks with the **bold** words in alphabetical order.

1. _____   7. _____

2. _____   8. _____

3. _____   9. _____

4. _____   10. _____

5. _____   11. _____

6. _____   12. _____

Bonus

CIRCLE the other words in the paragraph that have a long **e** sound.

✓ Check It!

Page 77

Keywords

1. actually	7. monkey
2. believe	8. mystery
3. chimney	9. teenager
4. creatures	10. thieves
5. energy	11. turkey
6. greenhouse	12. weasel

Bonus:

weirdest	sleep
dreams	knees
real	weak
dreamed	speak
these	finally
steal	

Page 78

Stack Up

Long E Spelled "Y"
1. energy
2. actually
3. mystery

Long E Spelled "EY"
1. chimney
2. monkey
3. turkey

Long E Spelled "EE"
1. teenager
2. greenhouse

Long E Spelled "EA"
1. creatures
2. weasel

Long E Spelled "IE"
1. believe
2. thieves

Page 79

Write It Right!

1. bel **i e** ve	6. f **e a** ture
2. Monk **e y** s	7. chimn **e y**
3. t **e e** nager	8. myster **y**
4. energ **y**	9. th **i e** f
5. ch **i e** f	10. pl **e a** se

Split It!

1. en•er•gy	6. li•brar•y
2. green•house	7. loy•al•ty
3. chim•ney	8. mem•o•ry
4. crea•ture	9. mys•ter•y
5. lib•er•ty	10. teen•ag•er

Stack Up

READ the keywords out loud. SORT them by how the long **e** sound is spelled.

actually	creatures	monkey	thieves
believe	energy	mystery	turkey
chimney	greenhouse	teenager	weasel

Long E, Spelled "Y"
Example: happy

1. _____

2. _____

3. _____

Long E, Spelled "EY"
Example: key

1. _____

2. _____

3. _____

Long E, Spelled "EE"
Example: meet

1. _____

2. _____

Long E, Spelled "EA"
Example: weak

1. _____

2. _____

Long E, Spelled "IE"
Example: retrieve

1. _____

2. _____

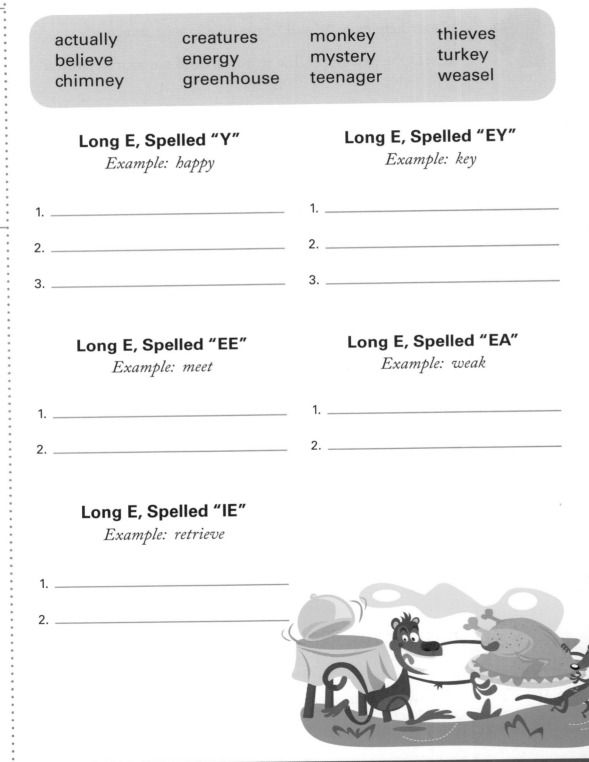

Write It Right!

FILL IN the missing letters to make the long **e** sound in each word.

Example: s __e__ __a__

1. I don't bel __~~i~~__ ve in ghosts!
2. Monk __y__ s live in the jungle.
3. My sister can't wait to be a t __e__ __e__ nager.
4. Turn off the lights to save energ __y__ .
5. Ty's dad is the ch __~~ei~~__ f of police.
6. People say my nose is my best f __~~ea~~__ ture.
7. Clean the chimn __e__ __y__ before having a fire in the fireplace.
8. I love to read a good myster ____ novel!
9. That squirrel is a th __e__ __i__ f! He stole my hot dog!
10. Always say "pl __e__ __s__ se" and "thank you."

(handwritten notes in margin: Belive / Beli / Cheirf / Cheit)

Split It!

SPLIT the keywords into syllables, using dots to mark the breaks.

Example: oodles   oo•dles

energy	1. _____	library	6. _____
greenhouse	2. _____	loyalty	7. _____
chimney	3. _____	memory	8. _____
creature	4. _____	mystery	9. _____
liberty	5. _____	teenager	10. _____

Spotlight on Plurals Again

Did you notice something weird about the words *monkeys* and *turkeys*? They're not spelled *monkies* and *turkies*. That's because when a word ends in "ey," you usually just add an "s" to make it plural. FILL IN the blanks with the plural of each word.

HINT: Check the ends of the words carefully.

Example: key   keys

Singular

Plural

monkey

1. _____

liberty

2. _____

knee

3. _____

chimney

4. _____

army

5. _____

library

6. _____

flea

7. _____

donkey

8. _____

jockey

9. _____

memory

10. _____

bumblebee

11. _____

journey

12. _____

mystery

13. _____

energy

14. _____

valley

15. _____

Word Search

FILL IN the blanks by solving the clues. CIRCLE the answers in the word grid. Words go down and across, not diagonally or backwards.

HINT: Remember to look for prefixes and suffixes.

Plural of **mystery**   1. _____

Past tense of **occupy**   2. _____

Plural of **ox**   3. _____

Adverb of **slight**   4. _____

Plural of **valley**   5. _____

Improve + "**-ing**"   6. _____

Plural of **flea**   7. _____

Lacking **value**   8. _____

One who **multiplies**   9. _____

Plural of **lullaby**   10. _____

Check It!

Page 81

Word Search

M	U	L	T	I	P	L	I	E	R	
O	C	C	U	P	I	E	D	A		F
V	A	L	L	E	Y	S	L	N		L
I	M	P	R	O	V	I	N	G		E
M	Y	S	T	E	R	I	E	S		A
O	N	E	T	B	R	S	O	L		S
X		S	L	I	G	H	T	L	Y	
E		L	U	L	L	A	B	I	E	S
N		V	A	L	U	E	L	E	S	S

Page 82

Spell Check

1. here	10. introduce
2. beautiful	11. breakdown
3. eight	12. education
4. argue	13. heartbeat
5. tonight	14. tulips
6. bright	15. rhyme
7. caboose	16. style
8. weighs	17. military
9. move	

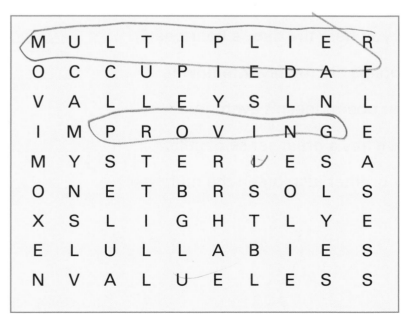

```
M U L T I P L I E R
O C C U P I E D A F
V A L L E Y S L N L
I M P R O V I N G E
M Y S T E R I E S A
O N E T B R S O L S
X S L I G H T L Y E
E L U L L A B I E S
N V A L U E L E S S
```

Spell Check

READ each sentence. CIRCLE the word that's misspelled. FILL IN the blanks with those misspelled words. Spell them right!

1. Come over hear and say that!   _____

2. What a beeyootiful necklace.   _____

3. I haven't seen Teena in ate days.   _____

4. Let's not argyoo about it.   _____

5. I can't wait for the party tonite!   _____

6. The stars are really brite in the sky.   _____

7. The last car on the train is the cabuse.   _____

8. Tariq ways himself on the scale.   _____

9. Don't moove! There's a bee in your hair.   _____

10. I want to introdyooce you to my friend.   _____

11. Our car had a brakedown yesterday.   _____

12. Everyone needs a good edyoocation.   _____

13. Do you hear the baby's heartbeet?   _____

14. Tyoolips are my favorite flower.   _____

15. That poem doesn't even rime.   _____

16. Olive has a great sense of stile.   _____

17. My brother just joined the militaree.   _____

Keywords

Remember the Oodles? Well, now let's meet their cousins, the Oodels and the Oodals.

READ the paragraph. The words in **bold** are your keywords.

When I went to the **hospital** to get my tonsils out, everyone was **gentle** and treated me like a **royal** visitor. I shared a **double** room with another kid and put my **personal** stuff in a **metal** locker. I wore a warm **flannel** bathrobe, slippers all day, and an ID bracelet with my name on the **label**. I got get-well cards from my class and the school **principal**. And my parents brought me almost a **barrel** of ice cream! I wrote all about it in my **journal**. The nurses called me a **model** patient, but I was very glad to go home!

FILL IN the blanks with the **bold** words in alphabetical order.

1. _____
2. _____
3. _____
4. _____
5. _____
6. _____

7. _____
8. _____
9. _____
10. _____
11. _____
12. _____

Stack Up

READ the keywords out loud. SORT them into the categories.

barrel	double	flannel	gentle	hospital	journal
label	metal	model	personal	principal	royal

Oodles
Example: tickle

1. _____

2. _____

Oodals
Example: medal

1. _____

2. _____

3. _____

4. _____

5. _____

6. _____

Oodels
Example: level

1. _____

2. _____

3. _____

4. _____

Criss Cross

FILL IN the grid by answering the clues with keywords.

ACROSS

1. A tag inside your clothes

4. A diary where you write your thoughts

5. Like a king, queen, or princess

6. A place filled with doctors

DOWN

2. A container for pickles, wine, or monkeys

3. A soft, warm fabric

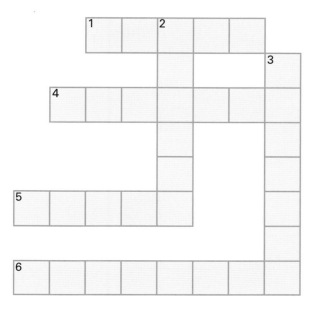

Mix & Match

In each box, MATCH a syllable on the left with a syllable on the right to make a word. DRAW a line between the two syllables to match them. REWRITE the words you matched in the blanks.

an	el	1. _____
lev	al	2. _____
wea	el	3. _____
trem	sel	4. _____
med	ble	5. _____
vow	gel	6. _____

crys	nel	7. _____
o	nal	8. _____
ped	tal	9. _____
fi	val	10. _____
tun	tel	11. _____
ho	al	12. _____

Word Blocks

FILL IN the word blocks with words of the same shape from the list.

angel	angle	barrel	brittle	label
ladle	general	personal	principal	principle

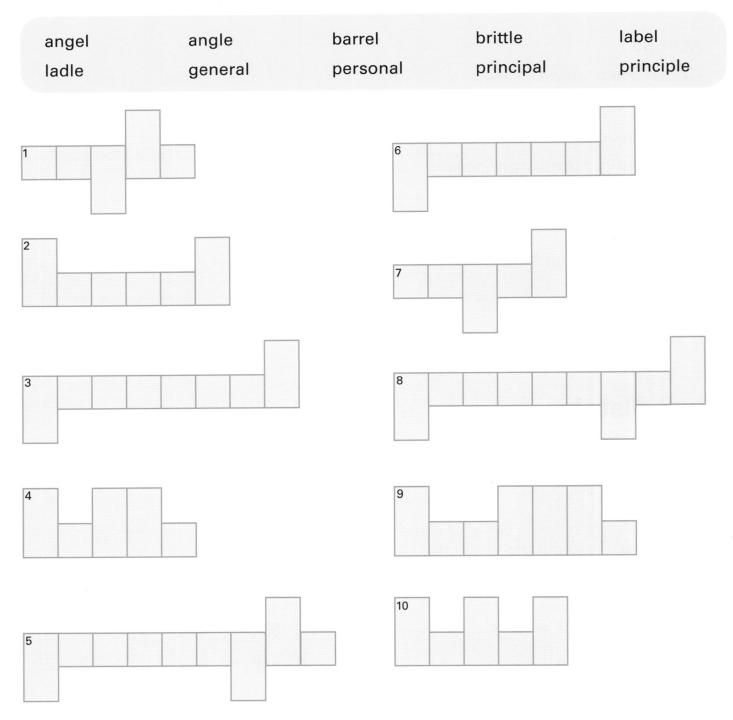

Keywords

No, you're not going crazy. Sometimes there are letters in words that you just don't hear. Three common silent letters are "k," "t," and "w."

READ the paragraph. The words in **bold** are your keywords.

I'm **writing** a story about a **knight**. One day, someone **knocked** on the door of his **castle**. It was an old lady asking for help. The knight refused to **listen**. The lady got on her **knees** and begged, but he slammed the door in her **wrinkled** face. The next day, the knight found a silk thread **knotted** around his fingers. He couldn't **unwrap** it, or even cut it with a **knife** or a **sword**. Now I need to write how he finds the **answer** to his problem. Got any ideas?

FILL IN the blanks with the **bold** words in alphabetical order.

1. _____

2. _____

3. _____

4. _____

5. _____

6. _____

7. _____

8. _____

9. _____

10. _____

11. _____

12. _____

✓ Check It!

Page 87

Keywords

1. answer
2. castle
3. knees
4. knife
5. knight
6. knocked
7. knotted
8. listen
9. sword
10. unwrap
11. wrinkled
12. writing

Page 88

Stack Up

"W" Is Silent
1. answer
2. sword
3. wrinkled
4. writing
5. unwrap

"K" Is Silent
1. knees
2. knife
3. knight
4. knocked
5. knotted

"T" Is Silent
1. castle
2. listen

Page 89

Spell Check

1. wrinkled
2. castle
3. writing
4. knotted
5. unwrap
6. answer
7. knocked
8. listen
9. knees
10. sword
11. knife
12. wrong
13. often

Page 90

Spotlight on Silent Letters

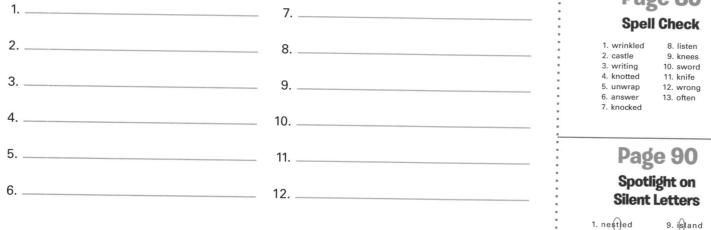

1. nestled
2. two
3. climb
4. whistle
5. sign
6. rhyme
7. ghost
8. Autumn
9. island
10. thumb
11. wrestles
12. whole
13. calf
14. wrench
15. knitted
16. soften

Stack Up

READ the keywords out loud. SORT them by their silent letters.

answer ✓   castle ✓   knees ✓   knife ✓
knight ✓   knocked ✓   knotted ✓   listen ✓
sword ✓   wrinkled ✓   writing ✓   unwrap ✓

"W" Is Silent

Example: wrong

1. answer
2. sword
3. wrinkled
4. writing
5. unrap

"K" Is Silent

Example: know

1. Knight
2. Knees
3. Knotted
4. Knocked
5. Knife

"T" Is Silent

Example: often

1. Castle
2. listen

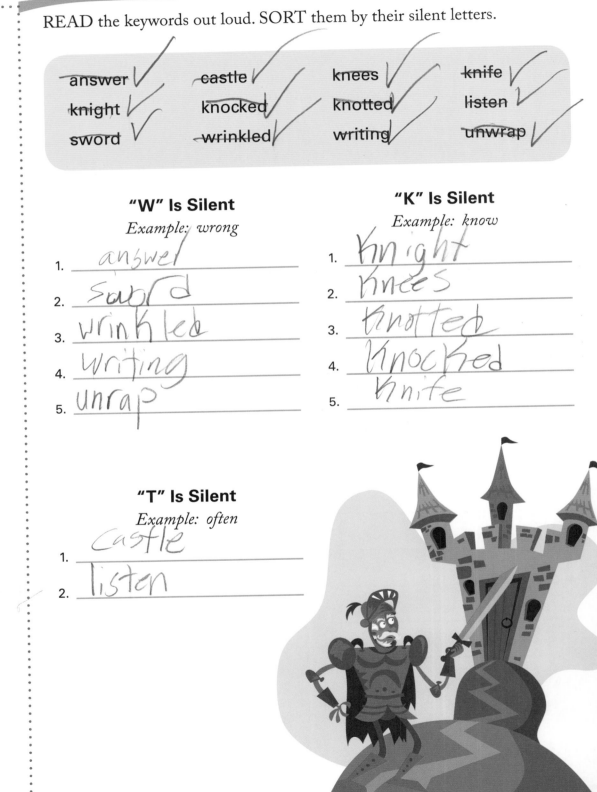

Spell Check

READ each sentence. CIRCLE the word that is misspelled. FILL IN the blanks with those misspelled words. Spell them right!

Handwritten answers: rinkled, castle, writing, knotted, unwrap, answer

1. My shirt is very (rinkled.)

2. I wish I lived in a fairy (cassle)

3. Jerome is good at (riting) stories.

4. Oh no! My shoelace is (notted) up.

5. We can't wait to (unrap) our gifts.

6. What's the (anser) to that question?

7. I (nocked) twice, but nobody was home.

8. Why doesn't anybody (lissen) to me?

9. My little sister has scabby (nees.)

10. A good knight always carries a (sord.)

11. Try cutting your meat with a (nife.)

12. My piano teacher hates (rong) notes.

13. I (offen) wonder if Shanice likes her new school.

Spotlight on Silent Letters

There are silent letters in many words. The easiest way to spot them is to look at the word, and then say it out loud. Give it a try! READ the sentences out loud. CIRCLE the silent letters in the **bold** words.

HINT: All the silents are consonants. Some words have two.

Example: I tied a knot in the string.

1. The kittens **nestled** near their mother.
2. I caught **two** fish today!
3. Did you **climb** that tree?
4. Coach is blowing his **whistle**.
5. Can't you read the **sign**?
6. It's time to **rhyme**.
7. You look like you've seen a **ghost**.
8. **Autumn** is my favorite season of the year.
9. We spent a week on a tropical **island**.
10. Oh! I got a paper cut on my **thumb**.
11. My Uncle Barry **wrestles** alligators.
12. Muriel ate the **whole** pie by herself.
13. The mama cow is feeding her **calf**.
14. You'll find a **wrench** in the toolbox.
15. Grandma **knitted** an ugly sweater for me.
16. I use lotion to **soften** my hands.

Keywords

The letter "n" sounds nice when it's on its own, but when it teams up with "k," it sounds a bit different.

READ the paragraph. The words in **bold** are your keywords.

On Mom's birthday, Dad gave her a bracelet of gold **links sprinkled** with diamonds that **twinkled** in the light. But Mom **ranks** number one in losing jewelry. She once dropped an emerald ring at the ice **rink**, snagged and broke an earring on her **pink** coat, and lost her favorite jade **monkey** necklace in the **trunk** of the car. Before you could **blink** your eyes, the birthday bracelet fell in the **sink**. She should keep her stuff at the **bank**! Next year, Dad's getting her nothing but **junk**, so it's okay if she loses it.

FILL IN the blanks with the **bold** words in alphabetical order.

1. _____
2. _____
3. _____
4. _____
5. _____
6. _____

7. _____
8. _____
9. _____
10. _____
11. _____
12. _____

✓ Check It!

Page 91

Keywords

1. bank
2. blink
3. junk
4. links
5. monkey
6. pink
7. ranks
8. rink
9. sink
10. sprinkled
11. trunk
12. twinkled

Page 92

Stack Up

Rhymes with *Think*	Rhymes with *Chunky*
1. blink	1. monkey
2. links	
3. pink	**Rhymes with *Tank***
4. rink	1. bank
5. sink	2. ranks

Rhymes with *Hunk*	Rhymes with *Wrinkled*
1. junk	1. sprinkled
2. trunk	2. twinkled

Page 93

Add It Up

1. wink   6. tank
2. stink   7. chunk
3. blink   8. drink
4. sink   9. rank
5. drank   10. prank

Bonus:
1. skunk   5. sank
2. flunk   6. honk
3. blank   7. wrinkle
4. yank

Page 94

Word Blocks

1. blanket
2. monkey
3. chunky
4. drinking
5. shrinking
6. thankful
7. wrinkle
8. sprinkle

Stack Up

READ the keywords out loud. SORT them by rhyme. FILL IN the blanks with the sorted words

bank	blink	junk	links	pink	monkey
ranks	rink	sink	sprinkled	trunk	twinkled

Rhymes with *Think(s)*
Example: wink

1. _____

2. _____

3. _____

4. _____

5. _____

Rhymes with *Tank(s)*
Example: blank

1. _____

2. _____

Rhymes with *Wrinkled*
Example: crinkled

1. _____

2. _____

Rhymes with *Hunk*
Example: sunk

1. _____

2. _____

Rhymes with *Chunky*
Example: spunky

1. _____

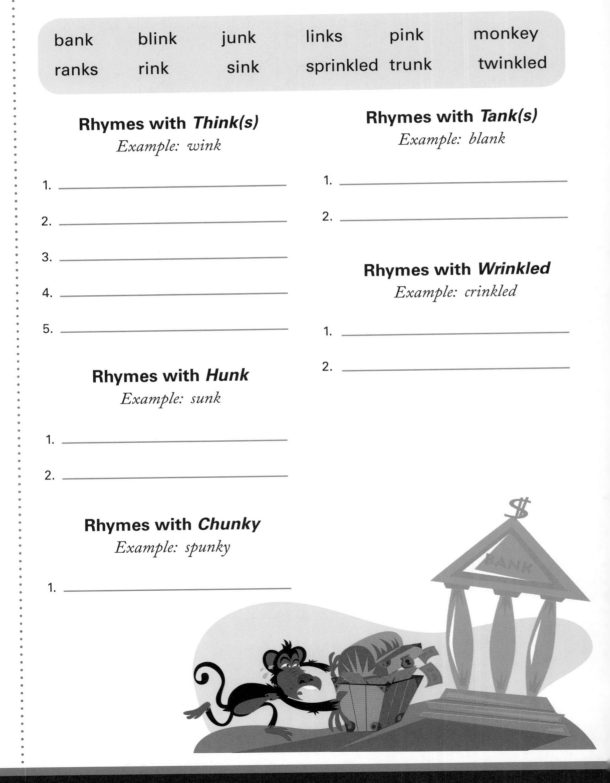

Add It Up

ADD or SUBTRACT the **bold** letter somewhere in the word to make a new word. FILL IN the blanks with the new words.

Example: fat + l = flat,   smart − s = mart

ink	+	w	=	1. _____
ink	+	st	=	2. _____
link	+	b	=	3. _____
stink	−	t	=	4. _____
rank	+	d	=	5. _____
thank	−	h	=	6. _____
hunk	+	c	=	7. _____
rink	+	d	=	8. _____
crank	−	c	=	9. _____
rank	+	p	=	10. _____

Bonus

You'll have to rearrange the letters to figure out these tricky ones!

sunk	+	k	=	1. _____
funk	+	l	=	2. _____
bank	+	l	=	3. _____
(bank − b)	+	y	=	4. _____
(sink − i)	+	a	=	5. _____
(hunk − u)	+	o	=	6. _____
(twinkle − t)	+	r	=	7. _____

Word Blocks

FILL IN the word blocks with words of the same shape from the list.

| wrinkle | thankful | blanket | sprinkle |
| chunky | monkey | drinking | shrinking |

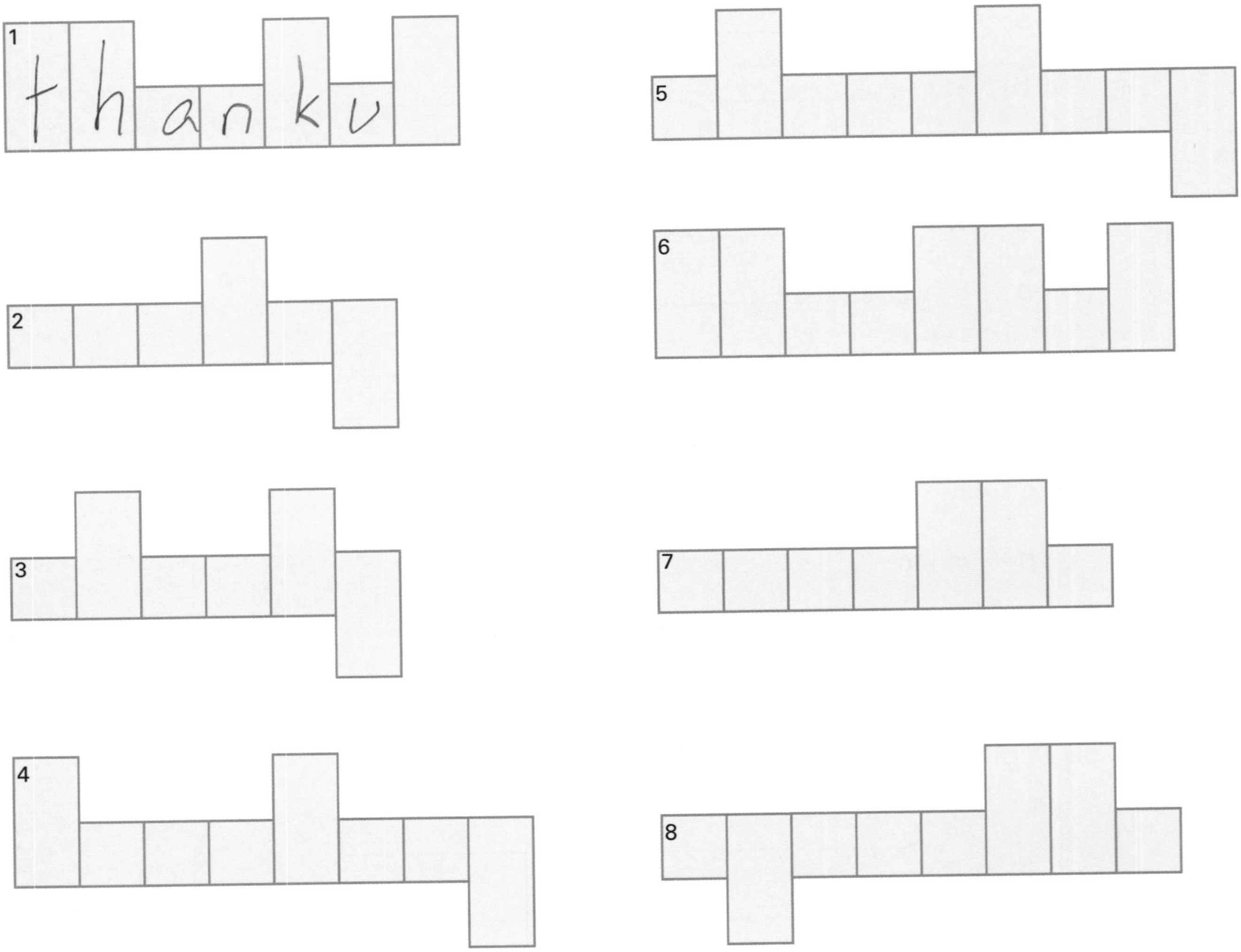

1 t h a n k u

2

3

4

5

6

7

8

Keywords

Sometimes, the letter "f" needs a break and brings in his friends "ph" and "gh" to do his work for him.

READ the paragraph. The words in **bold** are your keywords.

My friend Frank and I are working on a **graphic** novel, like a comic book. First it was about a **tough elephant** who falls in love with an **orphan dolphin**. But then we decided to make it about a **gopher** who's teaching his **nephew** the **alphabet**. When we talk on the **telephone**, Frank **laughs** so hard he starts to **cough**. Then his mom says we've had **enough** fun. Frank's a great friend!

FILL IN the blanks with the **bold** words in alphabetical order.

1. _____   7. _____

2. _____   8. _____

3. _____   9. _____

4. _____   10. _____

5. _____   11. _____

6. _____   12. _____

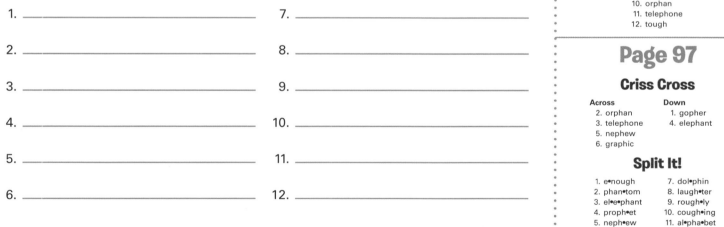

✓ Check It!

Page 95

Keywords

1. alphabet
2. cough
3. dolphin
4. elephant
5. enough
6. gopher
7. graphic
8. laughs
9. nephew
10. orphan
11. telephone
12. tough

Page 96

Write It Right!

1. alphabet
2. cough
3. dolphin
4. elephant
5. enough
6. gopher
7. graphic
8. laughs
9. nephew
10. orphan
11. telephone
12. tough

Page 97

Criss Cross

Across	Down
2. orphan	1. gopher
3. telephone	4. elephant
5. nephew	
6. graphic	

Split It!

1. e•nough	7. dol•phin
2. phan•tom	8. laugh•ter
3. el•e•phant	9. rough•ly
4. proph•et	10. cough•ing
5. neph•ew	11. al•pha•bet
6. go•pher	12. pheas•ant

✓ Check It!

Page 98

Spotlight on Silent "GH"

1. knight
2. caught
3. neighbors
4. fought
5. naughty
6. frighten
7. daughter
8. bought
9. taught
10. eight
11. stoplight
12. through
13. midnight

Write It Right!

REWRITE the misspelled keywords, using "ph" or "gh" instead of "f."

Example: rouf   *rough*

alfabet	1. _____
couf	2. _____
dolfin	3. _____
elefant	4. _____
enouf	5. _____
gofer	6. _____
grafic	7. _____
lafs	8. _____
nefew	9. _____
orfan	10. _____
telefone	11. _____
touf	12. _____

Criss Cross

FILL IN the grid by answering the clues with keywords.

ACROSS

2. A child with no parents

3. What you use to call your friends

5. The son of your sister or brother

6. Using pictures instead of words

DOWN

1. A small animal like a squirrel

4. Animal with a long trunk

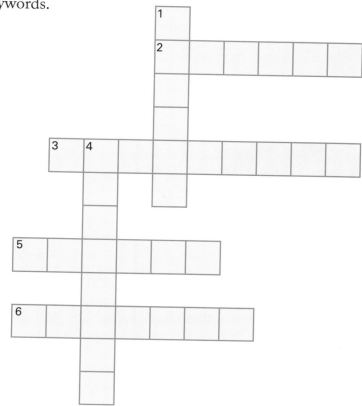

Split It!

SPLIT these words into syllables, using dots to mark the breaks.

HINT: READ each word out loud. LISTEN to the vowel in the first syllable.

Example: asleep   a•sleep

enough	1. _____	dolphin	7. _____
phantom	2. _____	laughter	8. _____
elephant	3. _____	roughly	9. _____
prophet	4. _____	coughing	10. _____
nephew	5. _____	alphabet	11. _____
gopher	6. _____	pheasant	12. _____

Spotlight on Silent "GH"

Most of the time, when you see "gh" in a word, you don't pronounce it at all. That's because it's helping the vowel. READ each sentence. CIRCLE the word that's missing a "gh." Then FILL IN the blank with the word. Put the "gh" back!

HINT: Check the ends of the words carefully.

Example: Turn out the (lit) and go to bed.   ___light___

He is a knit in shining armor.

Jamal caut the first fish.

The Patels are good neibors.

Ron and I fout about chores last week

Lissa was punished for being nauty.

Did that spider friten you?

Julio and his wife have a baby dauter.

Yesterday, Maria bout a new coat.

Greg taut me how to ride a bike.

There will be eit people at dinner.

There's a stoplit at that corner.

You can't drive throu that way.

On New Year's Eve, I stay up until midnit.

1. _____

2. _____

3. _____

4. _____

5. _____

6. _____

7. _____

8. _____

9. _____

10. _____

11. _____

12. _____

13. _____

Write It Right!

FILL IN the blanks with the missing letters of each word.

Example: I can't w<u>ai</u>t to go to Florida!

1. After practice, I go str _a_ _g_ _h_ _t_ t to my room.

2. My old bathing s ___ ___ t is so small, it's

   skint ___ ___ ___ t!

3. I started lifting w _e_ _i_ _g_ _h_ ts to get strong.

4. We drove through a tunn _e_ _l_ in the mountain.

5. Our car had a br _o_ ~~~~ kdown on the

   h _i_ _g_ _h_ way.

6. All of the army officers report to the gener ___ ___ .

7. My parents really like our n _e_ _i_ _g_ _h_ borhood.

8. Can you unscr _e_ _w_ the cap of the shamp _p_ _o_ ?

9. Little Gina is learning the al _p_ _b_ abet.

10. The smoke from the fire went up the chimn _e_ _y_ .

11. I have a c _o_ _u_ pon for five cents off a candy bar.

12. Dad puts lots of sugar on his grapefr ___ ___ t.

13. I get doub _l_ _e_ my allowance if I make dinner

    every night.

14. On Sundays, Mom puts my hair in br _a_ _i_ ds.

✓ Check It!

Page 99

Write It Right!

1. str <u>a i g h t</u>
2. s <u>u i t</u> / skint <u>i g h</u> t
3. w <u>e i g h</u> ts
4. tunn <u>e l</u>
5. br <u>e a</u> kdown / h <u>i g h</u> way
6. gener <u>a l</u>
7. n <u>e i g h</u> borhood
8. unscr <u>e w</u> / shamp <u>o o</u>
9. al <u>p h</u> abet
10. chimn <u>e</u> y
11. c <u>o u</u> pon
12. grapefr <u>u i t</u>
13. doub <u>l e</u>
14. br <u>a i</u> ds

Page 100

Stack Up

Long I Spelled "Y"
1. terrify
2. preoccupy
3. multiply
4. dragonfly

Long I Spelled "UE"
1. refuel
2. clueless
3. bluebells
4. untrue

Long E Spelled "Y"
1. memory
2. mystery
3. busybody
4. library

Has a Silent Letter
1. sandcastle
2. unwrapped
3. knocking
4. thumb

Stack Up

READ the words out loud. SORT them into these categories.
FILL IN the blanks with the sorted words.

unwrapped	library	thumb	terrify
refuel	mystery	preoccupy	sandcastle
memory	knocking	multiply	clueless
bluebells	dragonfly	busybody	untrue

Long I, Sound Spelled "Y"

1. _____
2. _____
3. _____
4. _____

Long U, Sound Spelled "UE"

1. _____
2. _____
3. _____
4. _____

Long E, Sound Spelled "Y"

1. _____
2. _____
3. _____
4. _____

Has a Silent Letter

1. _____
2. _____
3. _____
4. _____

Keywords

Some words, like *asleep*, aren't pronounced the way they're spelled. The "a" in *asleep* is not pronounced like an "a" because it isn't stressed. Instead, the "a" in *asleep* sounds like **uh**.

READ the paragraph. The words in **bold** are your keywords.

All **seven** of us went to the zoo. After we **arrived**, we **divided** into groups. My group went to see the **parrots** first. My brother's group headed straight for the **zebras** and lions. Mom went **alone** to the snakes **because** nobody else **appreciates** snakes. Eventually we **abandoned** the animals and ate **salads** for lunch. On the way home, we were **delayed** by traffic, so we all **pretended** to be our favorite animals to pass the time. What a great day!

FILL IN the blanks with the **bold** words in alphabetical order.

1. _____
2. _____
3. _____
4. _____
5. _____
6. _____
7. _____
8. _____
9. _____
10. _____
11. _____
12. _____

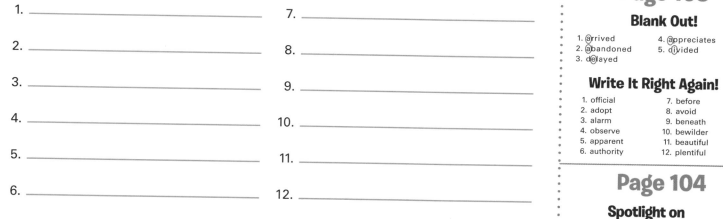

✓ **Check It!**

Page 101

Keywords

1. abandoned
2. alone
3. appreciates
4. arrived
5. because
6. delayed
7. divided
8. parrots
9. pretended
10. salads
11. seven
12. zebras

Page 102

Write It Right!

1. salads
2. because
3. seven
4. abandoned
5. zebras
6. arrived
7. delayed
8. alone
9. parrots
10. appreciates
11. divided
12. pretended

Page 103

Blank Out!

1. @rrived
2. @bandoned
3. d⊙layed
4. @ppreciates
5. d⊙vided

Write It Right Again!

1. official
2. adopt
3. alarm
4. observe
5. apparent
6. authority
7. before
8. avoid
9. beneath
10. bewilder
11. beautiful
12. plentiful

Page 104

Spotlight on UH-gain

1. accompany
2. addition
3. announced
4. arithmetic
5. arrange
6. arrested
7. aside
8. assured
9. attacked
10. aware
11. occasion
12. opinion
13. original
14. apartment
15. appeared

Write It Right!

REWRITE the misspelled keywords, using the correct vowel instead of "uh."

Example: uhsleep   asleep

sal**uh**ds

b**uh**cause

sev**uh**n

uhbandoned

zebr**uhs**

uhrrived

d**uh**layed

uhlone

parr**uh**ts

uhppreciates

d**uh**vided

pr**uh**tended

1. _____

2. _____

3. _____

4. _____

5. _____

6. _____

7. _____

8. _____

9. _____

10. _____

11. _____

12. _____

Blank Out!

FILL IN the blanks with keywords. CIRCLE the letter in each word that sounds like **uh**.

1. Our package _____ late but undamaged.

2. The stray puppy had been _____ by its owners.

3. Aunt Miriam's flight was _____ by bad weather.

4. Dad gets mad because nobody _____ his cooking.

5. We always _____ our holiday candy into three piles.

Write It Right Again!

REWRITE these misspelled words, using the correct vowel instead of "uh."

Example: happuhly   happily

uhfficial	1. _____
uhdopt	2. _____
uhlarm	3. _____
uhbserve	4. _____
uhpparent	5. _____
uhthority	6. _____
b**uh**fore	7. _____
uhvoid	8. _____
b**uh**neath	9. _____
b**uh**wilder	10. _____
beaut**uh**ful	11. _____
plent**uh**ful	12. _____

Spotlight on UH-gain

There are lots of words that start with **uh**. Can you spot them?

CIRCLE the word in each sentence that starts with the **uh** sound.

Example: I can't believe he did it (again!)

1. Will you accompany me on the piano?
2. We're building a new addition onto our house.
3. The judge announced the winners.
4. Is arithmetic the same thing as math?
5. Ronnie likes to arrange the flowers for the table.
6. I warned Celine that she'd be arrested for stealing!
7. Mr. Ling took me aside to tell me my painting was great.
8. Dad assured me that we would still go to the game.
9. The alligator attacked the men in the boat.
10. Are you even aware that I'm here?
11. Your birthday is a special occasion.
12. Tell me your opinion on football versus baseball.
13. The original recipe used butter, but Mom changed it.
14. Come on up to my apartment for dinner.
15. When spots appeared on my face, I knew I had chicken pox.

Keywords

Life is short. Who's got time for whole words? Instead of writing *I am*, we write *I'm*. And instead of saying *you will*, we say *you'll*, right? Words combined like that are called CONTRACTIONS. READ the paragraph. The words in **bold** are your keywords.

I'm sure **you've** heard it all before, but **here's** the problem: Mom will go into my room, and **she'll** start screaming because **there's** some stuff on the floor. It **isn't** the end of the world! **We've** been through this again and again. I **would've** cleaned my room, but I **don't** have the time. Mom just **doesn't** get it. I say, **let's** agree to disagree, **that's** all.

FILL IN the blanks with the **bold** words in alphabetical order.

1. _____
2. _____
3. _____
4. _____
5. _____
6. _____

7. _____
8. _____
9. _____
10. _____
11. _____
12. _____

✓ Check It!

Page 105

Keywords

1. doesn't
2. don't
3. here's
4. I'm
5. isn't
6. let's
7. she'll
8. that's
9. there's
10. we've
11. would've
12. you've

Page 106

Add It Up

1. there's
2. you've
3. here's
4. we've
5. doesn't
6. isn't
7. she'll
8. let's
9. that's
10. would've
11. don't

Page 107

Add It Up Again!

1. aren't
2. didn't
3. haven't
4. wouldn't
5. shouldn't

6. where's
7. they're
8. he's
9. he'll
10. we've

Pick the One!

1. shouldn't
2. wasn't
3. doesn't
4. haven't

5. there's
6. you've
7. aren't
8. couldn't

Page 108

Word Blocks

1. you've
2. doesn't
3. would've
4. she'll
5. they're
6. what's
7. didn't
8. aren't

Add It Up

FILL IN the blanks with the keyword that "solves the problem."

Example: I + am = I'm

there	+ is	=	1.	*there's*
you	+ have	=	2.	*you've*
here	+ is	=	3.	*here's*
we	+ have	=	4.	*we've*
does	+ not	=	5.	*dosn't*
is	+ not	=	6.	*isn't*
she	+ will	=	7.	*she'll*
let	+ us	=	8.	*let's*
that	+ is	=	9.	*that's*
would	+ have	=	10.	*would've*
do	+ not	=	11.	*don't*

DON'T
feed the bears!

Add It Up Again!

FILL IN the blanks with the contraction that "solves the problem."

HINT: The underlined letters get dropped.

Example: you + have = you've

are	+	n<u>o</u>t	=
did	+	n<u>o</u>t	=
have	+	n<u>o</u>t	=
would	+	n<u>o</u>t	=
should	+	n<u>o</u>t	=
where	+	<u>i</u>s	=
they	+	<u>a</u>re	=
he	+	<u>i</u>s	=
he	+	<u>wi</u>ll	=
we	+	<u>ha</u>ve	=

1. aren't
2. didn't
3. haven't
4. wouldn't
5. shouldn't
6. where's
7. they're
8. he's
9. he'll
10. we've

Pick the One!

Every contraction has this: '. It's called an APOSTROPHE, and it goes where the dropped letter used to be. CIRCLE the contraction that has the apostrophe in the right place.

Example: theyr'e (they're)

1. (shouldn't)   should'nt
2. was'nt   (wasn't)
3. does'nt   (doesn't)
4. (haven't)   have'nt

5. ther'es   (there's)
6. (you've)   youv'e
7. (aren't)   are'nt
8. could'nt   (couldn't)

Word Blocks

FILL IN the word blocks with words of the same shape from the list.

HINT: Watch for the apostrophes!

aren't   didn't   doesn't   she'll

they're   what's   would've   you've

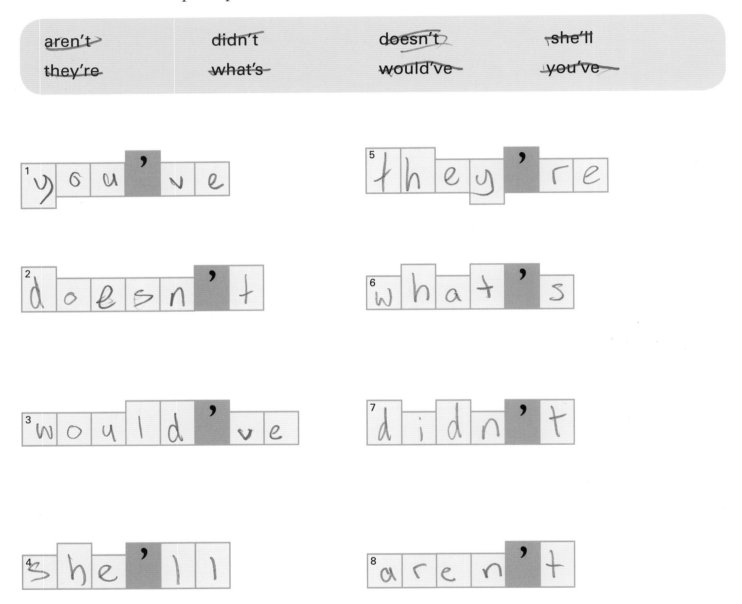

1. y o u ' v e

2. d o e s n ' t

3. w o u l d ' v e

4. s h e ' l l

5. t h e y ' r e

6. w h a t ' s

7. d i d n ' t

8. a r e n ' t

Keywords

Maybe the trickiest thing about spelling is that some words sound the same but are spelled differently. These words are called HOMOPHONES. Words like *write* and *right*, or *hear* and *here* are tricky. But not too tricky for YOU!

READ the paragraph. The words in **bold** are your keywords.

My older sister Theresa once tried to bake a **pear** tart. She did **not** do anything **right**! She was supposed to **pour** stuff into a bowl and **beat** it together, but it seemed like she just **threw flour** all over. When it was time to **break** the eggs, she dropped them instead. The **whole** kitchen was a mess. I **knew** mom **would** be mad for a **week**, so I helped Theresa clean up. She owes me one!

FILL IN the blanks with the **bold** words in alphabetical order.

1. beat
2. breat
3. flour
4. knew
5. not
6. pear
7. pour
8. right
9. threw
10. week
11. whole
12. would

✓ Check It!

Page 109

Keywords

1. beat
2. break
3. flour
4. knew
5. not
6. pear
7. pour
8. right
9. threw
10. week
11. whole
12. would

Page 110

Blank Out!

1. pear
2. week
3. flour
4. right
5. beat
6. knew
7. would
8. not
9. whole
10. break
11. threw
12. pour

Page 111

Spell Check

1. wood
2. new
3. poor
4. pair
5. break
6. write
7. week
8. hole
9. flower
10. not
11. beet
12. hear
13. where
14. there
15. right

Page 112

Blank Out!

1. threw, through
2. bee, be
3. blew, blue
4. planes, plains
5. tale, tail
6. Some, sum
7. stare, stair
8. whether, weather
9. they're, there
10. there, their
11. hour, our
12. sew, so
13. Hi, high
14. way, weigh
15. two, too
16. pause, paws

Blank Out!

FILL IN the blanks with the keyword that sounds like each word.

pair

weak

flower

write

beet

new

wood

knot

hole

brake

through

poor

1. _chair_
2. _week_
3. _power_
4. _right_
5. _beat_
6. _knew_
7. _could_
8. _not_
9. _whole_
10. _fake_
11. _t_
12. _for_

Spell Check

READ each sentence. CIRCLE the homophone that's wrong. *Write* the *right* homophone in the blank.

We burn would in our fireplace.

I love my knew video game!

Pour Joey lost his favorite jacket.

Luis got a cool pear of shoes.

We need a brake after all that work.

Aunt Sherri wants to right a novel.

Is your birthday next weak?

The chipmunk ran into a whole.

That flour smells so nice.

That is knot true at all.

Ick! I can't stand beat salad!

Did you here that sound?

Now wear did I put that towel?

I put it over they're.

Grace got every answer write.

1. _____

2. _____

3. _____

4. _____

5. _____

6. _____

7. _____

8. _____

9. _____

10. _____

11. _____

12. _____

13. _____

14. _____

15. _____

Homophones

Blank Out!

FILL IN the blanks with the right homophones.

through/threw

bee/be

blue/blew

planes/plains

tail/ tale

some/sum

stair/stare

weather/whether

there /they're

there/their

hour/our

so/sew

high/hi

way/weigh

two/too

paws/pause

1. Abby _____ a ball _____ the window.

2. If Dora was stung by a _____ , she would _____ sick.

3. We _____ bubbles until we were _____ in the face.

4. People fly in _____ over the Midwestern _____.

5. Mrs. Park tells a great _____ about a rat who lost its _____.

6. _____ kids can't stand to do a _____ on the board.

7. I felt everyone _____ at me as I stood on the top _____.

8. Did they say _____ the _____ would be good?

9. Hurry! I think _____ already _____.

10. The Jackson's new car is over _____, by _____house.

11. If we wait an _____, we can have _____ usual table.

12. You _____ clothes _____ nicely!

13. _____ there! Do you go to my _____ school?

14. What's the best _____ to _____ an elephant?

15. You _____ girls are much _____ sleepy to stay up.

16. The dogs _____ to lick their _____.

Keywords

Congratulations, you've spelled a lot of words! But there are always more. And some are really tough. Are you ready for a challenge?

READ the paragraph. The words in **bold** are your keywords.

Our neighbor, Ms. Cordero, has a smart family. Her son is a **scientist** who does **experiments** with **amphibians**, like frogs and **tortoises**. She has two **nieces** that play in a professional soccer **league**, but they're on **separate** teams. You would probably **recognize** her daughter, who's a famous actress. And her husband makes great cakes for special **occasions**! As for Ms. Cordero, she runs a company that **manufactures** MP3 players. Compared to the Corderos, my family seems lame. But that's not our **fault**. When you're around the Corderos, you're **surrounded** by geniuses!

FILL IN the blanks with the **bold** words in alphabetical order.

1. amphibians
2. experiments
3. fault
4. league
5. manufactures
6. nieces
7. occesions
8. recognize
9. scientist
10. separate
11. surrounded
12. tortoises

✔ **Check It!**

Page 113

Keywords

1. amphibians
2. experiments
3. fault
4. league
5. manufactures
6. nieces
7. occasions
8. recognize
9. scientist
10. separate
11. surrounded
12. tortoises

Page 114

Split It!

1. au•thor•i•ty
2. a•rith•me•tic
3. an•nounce
4. ac•com•pa•ny
5. ex•per•i•ment
6. man•u•fac•ture
7. oc•ca•sion
8. rec•og•nize
9. sci•en•tist
10. sep•a•rate
11. sur•round
12. tor•toise

Page 115

Criss Cross

Across
3. scientist
4. manufactures
6. surrounded
7. separate

Down
1. occasions
2. nieces
5. recognize

Split It!

SPLIT these words into syllables, using dots to mark the breaks.

authority	1. _____
arithmetic	2. _____
announce	3. _____
accompany	4. _____
experiment	5. _____
manufacture	6. _____
occasion	7. _____
recognize	8. _____
scientist	9. _____
separate	10. _____
surround	11. _____
tortoise	12. _____

✓ Check It!

Page 116

Stack Up

Words with Doubles
1. bul•le•tin
2. hip•po•pot•a•mus
3. im•me•di•ate•ly
4. op•po•site
5. suf•fi•cient
6. im•pos•si•ble

Words with No Doubles
1. bal•ance
2. ben•e•fit
3. col•o•ny
4. lin•en
5. op•er•a•tion
6. sal•a•man•der

Criss Cross

FILL IN the grid by answering the clues with keywords.

ACROSS

3. Someone who knows a lot about plants or chemicals

4. Builds in a factory

6. Enclosed on all sides

7. Disconnected, not shared

DOWN

1. Events or celebrations

2. Your brother's daughters are your ___.

5. To know by sight

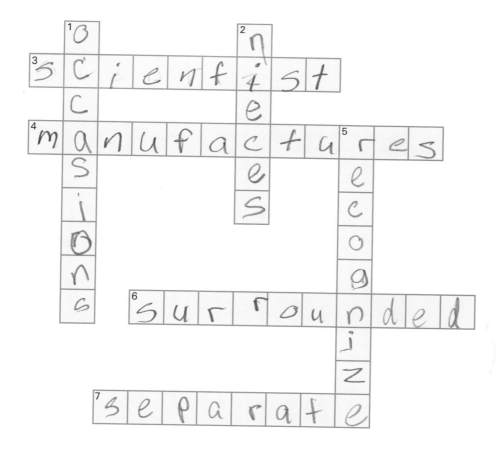

Stack Up

Time for a flashback. Remember syllables and double consonants? If a syllable has a short vowel sound, it probably ends in a consonant. And you usually split a double consonant between the double letters.

SORT these words by doubles and no doubles.
SPLIT the words into syllables, using dots to mark the breaks.

balance	benefit	bulletin	colony
hippopotamus	immediately	linen	opposite
operation	salamander	sufficient	impossible

Words with Doubles
Example: op•por•tu•ni•ty

1. _____

2. _____

3. _____

4. _____

5. _____

6. _____

Words with No Doubles
Example: mel•on

1. _____

2. _____

3. _____

4. _____

5. _____

6. _____

Word Blocks

FILL IN the word blocks with words of the same shape from the list.

HINT: Watch for the apostrophes!

brightly	couldn't	endless	miscount
prepaid	recycle	subtotal	swiftness
their	they're	unhappy	wasn't

✓ Check It!

Page 117
Word Blocks

1. couldn't
2. brightly
3. subtotal
4. miscount
5. they're
6. swiftness
7. prepaid
8. endless
9. recycle
10. wasn't
11. unhappy
12. their

Page 118
Spell Check

1. scientist
2. hottest
3. settle
4. stitches
5. recognize
6. butterflies
7. You've
8. shopping
9. smiling
10. politely
11. helpful
12. preheat
13. impossible
14. mice
15. niece
16. tortoise
17. wouldn't

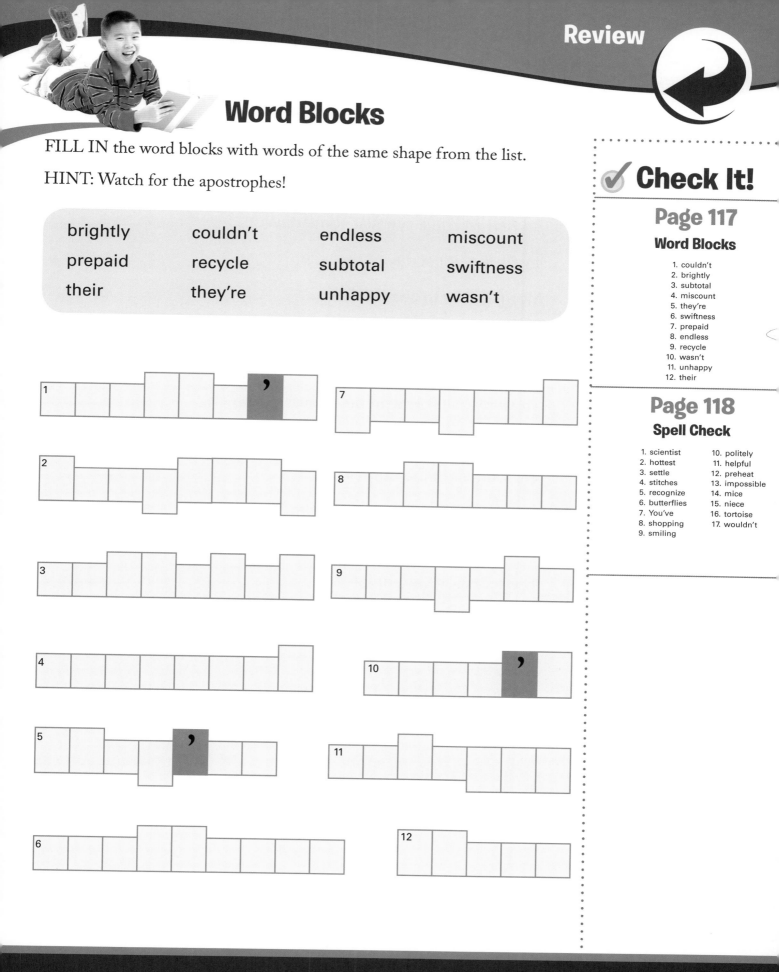

Spell Check

READ each sentence. CIRCLE the word that's misspelled. FILL IN the blanks with those misspelled words. Spell them right!

Brynne will be a syentist some day.

1. _____

It was the hotist day of the year.

2. _____

Mom told us to settuhl down.

3. _____

Terence needed three stichiz in his arm.

4. _____

No one will recuhgnyze you in that mask.

5. _____

The air was filled with butterflys.

6. _____

Yoo've got a pimple on your nose.

7. _____

We went shoping at the mall.

8. _____

I don't know why you're smileing.

9. _____

Mom always says to ask politeley.

10. _____

The hints are very helpfull.

11. _____

The box says to preeheat the oven.

12. _____

Travel through time? That's imposible!

13. _____

My dog is good at catching mouses.

14. _____

Amy's not her daughter, she's her knees.

15. _____

You are as slow as a tortuss.

16. _____

Woulden't you like to know?

17. _____

abandoned	children	families	hikes	melt
actually	chimney	fault	holiday	men
afternoon	choose	fearless	holler	metal
alone	churches	fields	hooves	mice
alphabet	cities	final	hospital	middle
amphibians	clapped	finally	hugging	misbehave
answer	cleaner	finest	hurry	misinformed
answers	closely	firelight	I'm	misleading
appreciates	closer	flannel	inches	model
approve	cloudless	flopped	invited	monkey
arrived	clue	flour	isn't	moved
babies	communities	flowers	journal	multiply
backyard	companies	follow	joyful	mystery
bank	completely	football	juice	neatest
barefoot	cooks	foxes	junk	needle
barrel	costume	fright	kitten	neighbors
baseball	cough	geese	knees	nephew
basket	countries	gentle	knew	nicer
beat	coupon	gentler	knife	nieces
because	creatures	gopher	knight	not
begged	cupcake	grabbed	knocked	occasions
believe	darkness	grandmother	knotted	occupy
birthday	delayed	grapefruit	label	oldest
blink	delightful	graphic	lady	orphan
bodies	deny	grateful	largest	outside
boils	divided	great	laughs	overnight
break	doesn't	greenhouse	league	oxen
bridle	dolphin	greets	let's	parrots
bunches	don't	grills	links	pear
calmer	double	gripped	listen	perfectly
calves	eight	group	lives	personal
candle	elephant	handful	loaves	pillow
careless	energy	handle	longer	pink
carry	enough	happiest	lullaby	pinned
castle	experiments	happily	lunches	planning
cattle	fabric	here's	mainly	play
chicken	factories	heroes	manufactures	plentiful

Spelling Words Index

3rd-Grade Vocabulary Success

Keywords

ac•quire—uh-KWIR *verb* 1. to get as your own 2. to gain for yourself
Synonyms: get, gain, obtain. Antonyms: provide, give.

e•nor•mous—ih-NAWR-muhs *adjective* unusually large in size or number
Synonyms: huge, massive, gigantic. Antonyms: tiny, small.

frac•ture—FRAK-cher *verb* to break
Synonyms: break, crack, rupture. Antonyms: fix, mend.

gloom•y—GLOO-mee *adjective* 1. dark 2. sad
Synonyms: dark, unhappy, sad. Antonyms: bright, cheerful.

hu•mor•ous—HYOO-mer-uhs *adjective* funny
Synonyms: amusing, hilarious, funny. Antonyms: serious.

in•quire—ihn-KWIR *verb* to ask about
Synonyms: ask, request. Antonyms: respond.

mend—mehnd *verb* 1. to fix 2. to make better
Synonyms: repair, fix, recover. Antonyms: break, fracture.

mi•nus•cule—MIHN-uh-skyool *adjective* very small
Synonyms: tiny, minute, little. Antonyms: enormous, gigantic.

pro•vide—pruh-VID *verb* 1. to take care of 2. to supply what is needed
Synonyms: give, offer, supply. Antonyms: get, take.

re•spond—rih-SPAHND *verb* 1. to answer 2. to react in response
Synonyms: reply, answer. Antonyms: ask, question.

✓ Check It!

Page 124

Read and Replace

1. respond
2. mend
3. provide
4. enormous
5. fracture
6. minuscule
7. gloomy
8. acquire
9. inquire
10. humorous

Page 125

Petal Power

1. gloomy
2. provide
3. inquire
4. enormous

Page 126

Tic-Tac-Toe

1. reply, answer, tell
2. mend, connect, attach
3. sad, grim, depressing
4. collect, earn, gain

Page 127

Criss Cross

ACROSS	DOWN
1. inquire	2. respond
4. mend	3. enormous
6. gloomy	5. minuscule
7. humorous	8. fracture
9. provide	
10. acquire	

Read & Replace

READ the letter. Each word in **bold** is a SYNONYM to a keyword. Synonyms are words that have the same meanings, like *broad* and *wide*. FILL IN the blanks using a keyword from the word box.

| acquire | enormous | fracture | gloomy | humorous |
| inquire | mend | minuscule | provide | respond |

Dear Ms. Trainer,

I am writing this to 1 _____ to your e-mail. I'm sorry to hear

reply

your elephant has a broken bone. I wish that I could help you

2 _____ your elephant's leg. Unfortunately I do not have

fix

a cast to 3 _____ you. My company does not make casts

give

for 4 _____ animals when they 5 _____ a bone. Most

very large   break

people can tell by our company name that we only make casts

for 6 _____ creatures.

tiny

I know this must be a 7 _____ time for you. I hope you will

sad

8 _____ the cast you need soon. You might want to contact

get

the Jumbo Cast Company to 9 _____ about a cast.

ask

Sincerely,

Dr. Bones, President

Itsy Bitsy Cast Company

P.S. I don't mean to be 10 _____ at such

funny

a serious time, but if you do ever need a

cast for any of the fleas at your circus, I'd be

happy to help.

Petal Power

The petals around the flowers are ANTONYMS to the word in the center. Antonyms are words that have opposite meanings, like *tiny* and *huge*. READ the words around each flower and WRITE an antonym from the keywords in the center.

enormous   gloomy   inquire   mend   provide

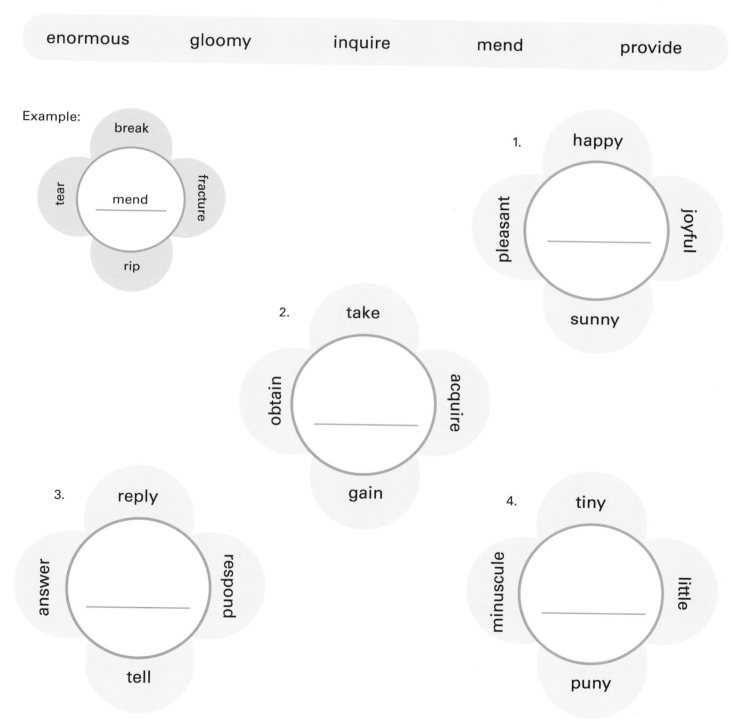

Example:

break
tear   mend   fracture
rip

1. happy
pleasant   _____   joyful
sunny

2. take
obtain   _____   acquire
gain

3. reply
answer   _____   respond
tell

4. tiny
minuscule   _____   little
puny

Tic-Tac-Toe

PLAY Tic-tac-toe with synonyms and antonyms. CIRCLE any word that is a synonym to the blue word. PUT an X through any antonyms. When you find three synonyms or antonyms in a row, you are a winner! The line can go across, down, or horizontally.

Example:

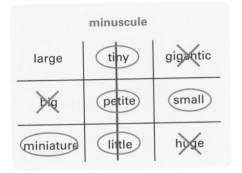

1. respond

reply	ask	question
ignore	answer	inquire
react	request	tell

2. fracture

break	fix	mend
crack	shatter	connect
join	tear	attach

3. humorous

sad	comical	funny
serious	grim	laughable
hilarious	unfunny	depressing

4. acquire

give	get	gain
lose	earn	sell
collect	provide	buy

Criss Cross

FILL IN the grid by writing keywords that are synonyms to the clues.

ACROSS

1. To ask

4. To fix

6. Dark or sad

7. Funny

9. To give something to someone

10. To get something for yourself

DOWN

2. To answer

3. Very big

5. Tiny

8. To break

Synonyms & Antonyms

Blank Out!

FILL IN the blanks with keywords.

acquire	enormous	fracture	gloomy	humorous
inquire	mend	minuscule	provide	respond

1. Kendra ripped her shirt climbing the rock wall. Now she'll have to _____ it.

2. If you hit a baseball through the window, you will _____ the glass.

3. The ring leader will _____ red noses to all the students at clown school.

4. It took hours for Jack and Liz to finish their _____ tub of popcorn.

5. Anna will _____ and find out if the mountain is open for snowboarding.

6. It's a _____ day when your best friend moves away.

7. We had to use a microscope to see the _____ creatures living in the pond water.

8. My brother wrote a _____ e-mail that made my parents laugh out loud.

9. If Kate can just _____ the two trading cards she needs, she'll have a complete collection.

10. Max wants everyone to _____ to the birthday party invitation so he'll know how much cake to make.

Night & Day

MATCH each word in the moon column to its antonym in the sun column.

HINT: If you don't know the meaning of a word, look it up in a dictionary or thesaurus.

1. enormous _____   a. bright

2. provide _____   b. destroy

3. humorous _____   c. query

4. minuscule _____   d. seize

5. respond _____   e. microscopic

6. acquire _____   f. answer

7. fracture _____   g. dismal

8. mend _____   h. humongous

9. gloomy _____   i. hand over

10. inquire _____   j. meld

Synonyms & Antonyms

Blank Out!

FILL IN in the blanks with keywords.

acquire	enormous	fracture	gloomy	humorous
inquire	mend	minuscule	provide	respond

1. A mountain and a blue whale are both _____.

2. To find out if your friend is busy, you have to _____.

3. The sky is _____ when it's full of dark clouds.

4. When you fix your torn jacket, you _____ it.

5. The size of a period at the end of a sentence is _____.

6. When you get a new bike, you _____ it.

7. If you don't wear a helmet and pads when you're skateboarding, you could _____ a bone.

8. A funny joke is _____.

9. When you answer a friend's e-mail, you _____ to it.

10. When your parents give you everything you need, they _____ for you.

 **Check It!**

Cut out the Check It! section on page 123, and see if you got the answers right.

Keywords

ap•proach—uh-PROHCH *verb* 1. to move closer to 2. to speak to someone in order to ask something
Synonyms: advance, move toward. Antonyms: retreat, pull back.

ben•e•fi•cial—behn-uh-FIHSH-uhl *adjective* 1. helpful 2. leading to good health and happiness
Synonyms: helpful, useful. Antonyms: harmful, destructive.

grad•u•al—GRAJ-ooh-uhl *adjective* moving or changing slowly in steps or degrees
Synonyms: slow, steady, regular. Antonyms: sudden, fast.

im•prove—ihm-PROOV *verb* to make or become better
Synonyms: get better, recover. Antonyms: worsen, deteriorate.

lo•cate—LOH-kayt *verb* 1. to find where something is 2. to put in a particular spot
Synonyms: place, find, discover. Antonyms: lose, misplace.

man•u•fac•ture—man-yuh-FAK-cher *verb* to make by hand or with machinery
Synonyms: make, produce, create. Antonyms: destroy, demolish.

o•rig•i•nal—uh-RIHJ-uh-nuhl *adjective* 1. existing first 2. completely new and not copied
Synonyms: first, earliest, new. Antonyms: final, copy.

suf•fi•cient—suh-FIHSH-uhnt *adjective* as much as needed
Synonyms: enough, plenty, ample. Antonyms: inadequate, poor.

un•lim•it•ed—uhn-LIH-mih-tuhd *adjective* 1. without limits 2. having no boundaries or end
Synonyms: boundless, limitless. Antonyms: confined, bound.

van•ish—VAN-ihsh *verb* 1. to disappear suddenly 2. to stop existing
Synonyms: disappear, go. Antonyms: appear, show.

✓ Check It!

Page 132

Read & Replace

1. approach
2. vanish
3. gradual
4. improve
5. original
6. locate
7. manufacture
8. sufficient
9. beneficial
10. unlimited

Page 133

Petal Power

1. gradual
2. beneficial
3. original
4. locate
5. unlimited

Page 134

Tic-Tac-Toe

1. harm, hurt, worsen
2. build, construct, form
3. appear, arrive, show up
4. lacking, short of, skimpy

Page 135

Criss Cross

ACROSS
2. improve
3. vanish
6. approach
7. gradual
9. unlimited

DOWN
2. original
4. locate
5. manufacture
8. sufficient

Check It!

Page 136

Blank Out!

1. improve
2. manufacture
3. approach
4. locate
5. beneficial
6. vanish
7. sufficient
8. gradual
9. unlimited
10. original

Page 137

Night & Day

1. h
2. j
3. a
4. b
5. c
6. d
7. i
8. e
9. g
10. f

Page 138

Blank Out!

1. vanish
2. improve
3. locate
4. sufficient
5. manufacture
6. beneficial
7. approach
8. unlimited
9. gradual
10. original

Read & Replace

READ the e-mail. Each word or phrase in **bold** is a SYNONYM to a keyword. Synonyms are words that have the same meanings, like *big* and *large*. FILL IN the blanks with keywords.

approach	beneficial	gradual	improve	locate
manufacture	original	sufficient	unlimited	vanish

From: Farmer Brown

To: Mr. Mysterio

Subject: My Missing Pet

Your assistant gave me your e-mail address so I could

1 _____ you with my problem. Yesterday I watched
   come to

as you made my potbellied pig 2 _____. It was not a
                                  disappear

3 _____ disappearance—she was gone with a snap of
   bit-by-bit

your fingers. That was quite a trick! I understand that you wanted

to 4 _____ your 5 _____ magic show. Unfortunately,
      better   *first*

I still cannot 6 _____ Petunia.
                  find

Thank you for your offer to 7 _____ a new pet
                               make

for me. However, I do not think a pink balloon

poodle would be a 8 _____ replacement
                     good enough

for Petunia. Any advice you can give me

would be 9 _____. I have
            helpful

10 _____ love for my pet.
    endless

Petal Power

The petals around the flowers are ANTONYMS to the word in the center. Antonyms are words that have opposite meanings, like *hot* and *cold*. Read the words around each flower and WRITE an antonym from the keywords list in the center.

beneficial   gradual   locate   original   unlimited

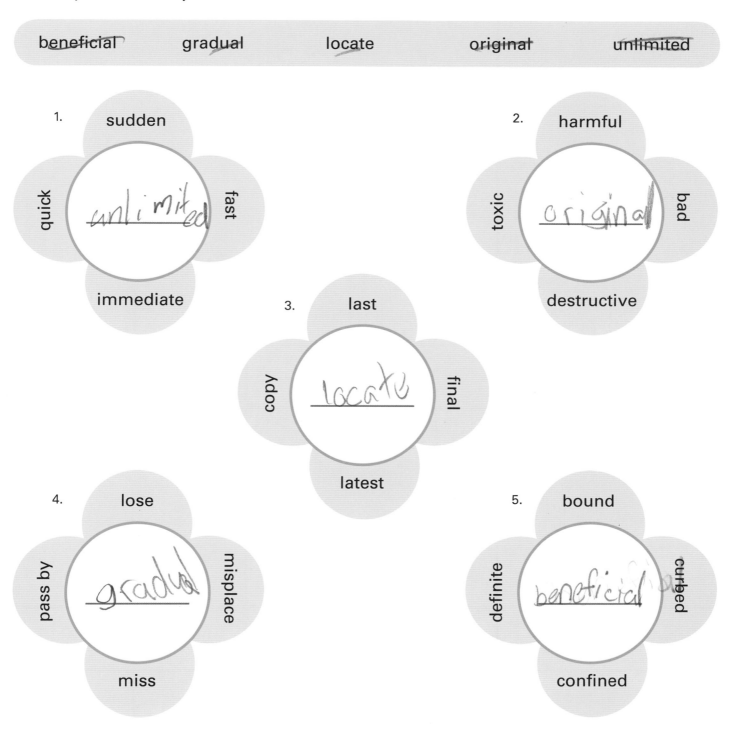

1. sudden
quick   *unlimited*   fast
immediate

2. harmful
toxic   *original*   bad
destructive

3. last
copy   *locate*   final
latest

4. lose
pass by   *gradual*   misplace
miss

5. bound
definite   *beneficial*   curbed
confined

Tic-Tac-Toe

PLAY Tic-tac-toe with synonyms and antonyms. CIRCLE any word that is a synonym to the blue word. PUT an X through any antonyms. When you find three synonyms or antonyms in a row, you are a winner! The line can go across, down, or diagonally.

Example:

approach		
come at	go to	meet
greet	take off	go away
leave	move toward	depart

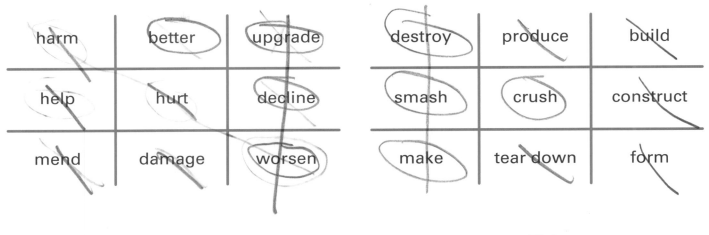

1. improve

harm	better	upgrade
help	hurt	decline
mend	damage	worsen

2. manufacture

destroy	produce	build
smash	crush	construct
make	tear down	form

3. vanish

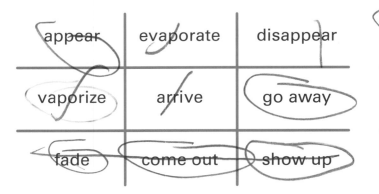

appear	evaporate	disappear
vaporize	arrive	go away
fade	come out	show up

4. sufficient

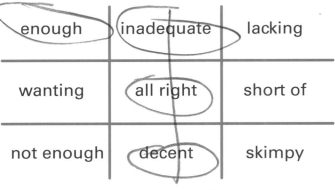

enough	inadequate	lacking
wanting	all right	short of
not enough	decent	skimpy

Criss Cross

FILL IN the grid by writing keywords that are synonyms to the clues.

ACROSS

1. To get better
3. To disappear
6. To advance
7. Slowly
9. Countless

DOWN

2. Earliest
4. To discover
5. To construct
8. Enough

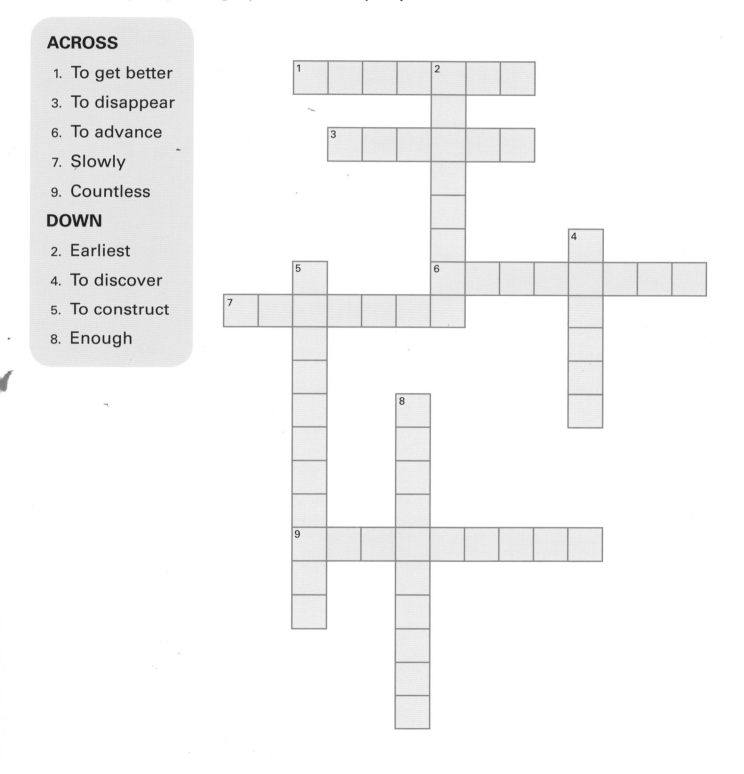

Blank Out!

FILL in the blanks with keywords.

approach	beneficial	gradual	improve	locate
manufacture	original	sufficient	unlimited	vanish

1. Taylor practiced at the skate park so she could _____ her pipe grind.

2. They _____ candy canes from water and sugar.

3. Shayna will _____ the singer after the show to ask for his autograph.

4. It took hours for Max to _____ his hamster after it escaped from its cage.

5. It would be _____ to put Brad's bike in the garage before the storm hits.

6. Casey watched her chalk drawing _____ in the rain.

7. Please make sure to order a _____ amount of pizza for the party.

8. The tide will make a _____ move up the beach, so we should move our towels.

9. Darren has an _____ pass to the amusement park this year so he can go anytime he wants.

10. The _____ surfboards were made from wood. Now they're mostly made with fiberglass.

Night & Day

MATCH each word in the moon column to its antonym in the sun column.

1. unlimited   _____

2. gradual   _____

3. sufficient   _____

4. manufacture   _____

5. locate   _____

6. approach   _____

7. vanish   _____

8. beneficial   _____

9. improve   _____

10. original   _____

a. wanting

b. destroy

c. misplace

d. leave

e. damaging

f. copy

g. worsen

h. limited

i. appear

j. rapid

Blank Out!

FILL in the blanks with keywords.

approach	beneficial	gradual	improve	locate
manufacture	original	sufficient	unlimited	vanish

1. When you blow out your birthday candles, the flames _____.

2. If you want to be a better dancer, you need to _____.

3. To find your lost baseball card, you need to _____ it.

4. If you want to buy a 75-cent candy bar, a dollar is _____.

5. People who work in a car factory _____ cars.

6. Flippers are _____ to a swimmer.

7. When dogs want to sniff your hand, they _____ you.

8. The number of stars you can see in the sky is _____.

9. The speed at which your hair grows is _____.

10. Your very first bicycle is your _____ bicycle.

Check It!

Cut out the Check It! section on page 131, and see if you got the answers right.

Keywords

bare—behr *adjective* 1. naked 2. exposed for all to see 3. empty

bear—behr *noun* a large mammal that has long shaggy hair and a short tail and eats both plants and meat
verb 1. to hold up something heavy 2. to keep in one's mind

fair—fehr *noun* 1. a gathering of people who are buying and selling things 2. an event with rides, games, and competitions
adjective 1. beautiful 2. clean or pure 3. not stormy or cloudy 4. likely to happen 5. not dark 6. neither good nor bad 7. in a way that is equal for everyone involved

fare—fehr *noun* 1. food 2. the money a person pays to travel by public transportation

heal—heel *verb* to make healthy

heel—heel *noun* 1. the back part of the foot below the ankle 2. the part of a shoe that covers the back of the foot 3. the lower, back, or end part 4. a person who is not nice
verb to make a person or animal obey

scent—sehnt *noun* 1. an odor or smell 2. a sense of smell 3. hint 4. perfume

sent—sehnt *verb* 1. caused to go 2. caused to happen

weak—week *adjective* not strong

week—week *noun* the period of seven days that begins with Sunday and ends with Saturday

✓ Check It!

Page 140

Read & Replace

1. bear
2. bare
3. week
4. weak
5. sent
6. fair
7. fare
8. heal
9. heel
10. scent

Page 141

Homophone Hopscotch

Board 1	Board 2	Board 3
1. fair	1. heel	1. bare
2. fare	2. heel	2. bear
3. fair	3. heel	3. bear
4. fare	4. heal	4. bare
5. fair	5. heel	5. bare

Page 142

It's Puzzling!

A. fair/I. fare
B. week/G. weak
C. bear/J. bare
D. heel/F. heal
E. scent/H. sent

Page 143

Criss Cross

ACROSS	DOWN
1. weak	1. week
2. heel	2. heal
3. bear	3. bare
4. fair	4. fare
5. scent	5. sent

Read & Replace

HOMOPHONES are words that sound the same but have different meanings. *Too*, *two*, and *to* are homophones. READ the story. FILL IN the blanks with keywords.

HINT: Read the whole story before you choose your words.

bear	fare	heel	sent	week
bare	fair	heal	scent	weak

This morning, I heard Mom yell, "Henry, you had better not be going out in your 1_____ feet!" I said, "Mom, I love my big, furry clawed slippers. Would you rather me go out without anything on my 2_____ feet?"

The slippers came in the mail last 3_____. They were a present from my Great Aunt Irma. She may look 4_____, but once she hit a baseball so hard she 5_____ it flying to the next town. Great Aunt Irma is a lot of fun. We always go to the county 6_____ together, and she even pays the bus 7_____ for me. She sells a magic cream at the fair that can 8_____ any toothache if you rub it on your 9_____. Great Aunt Irma puts a drop of skunk 10_____ into every batch. I love my Great Aunt Irma a lot, but I would never ever buy her toothache cream!

Stinky Skunk Toothache Cream

Homophone Hopscotch

LOOK AT the clues for each hopscotch board. MATCH each space on the board to its clue. Then FILL IN the correct keyword.

Board 1: fair/fare
1. beautiful
2. price to ride a train
3. a place where people buy and sell things
4. food
5. in a way that's equal for everyone

Board 2: heal/heel
1. a person who is not nice
2. the back part of the foot
3. the end part
4. to make better
5. to make an animal obey

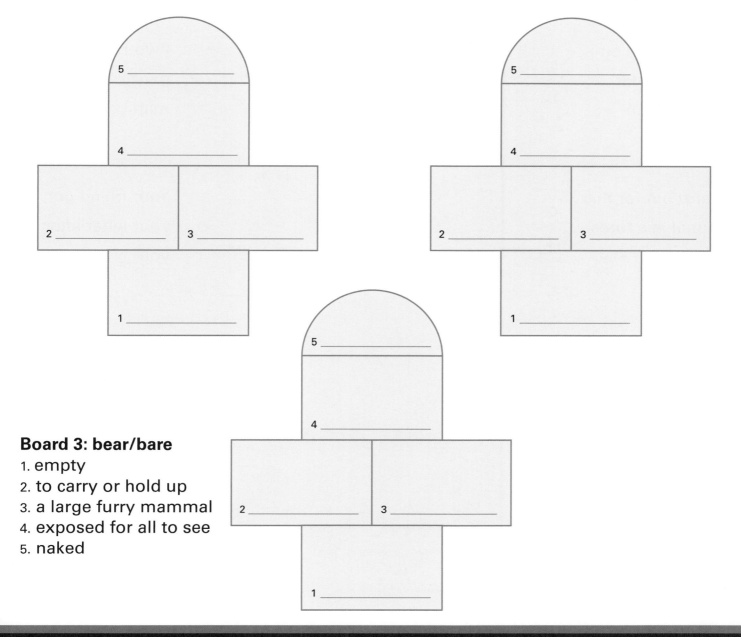

Board 3: bear/bare
1. empty
2. to carry or hold up
3. a large furry mammal
4. exposed for all to see
5. naked

It's Puzzling!

FILL IN a keyword to solve each clue. Then DRAW a line from each puzzle piece to its homophone partner.

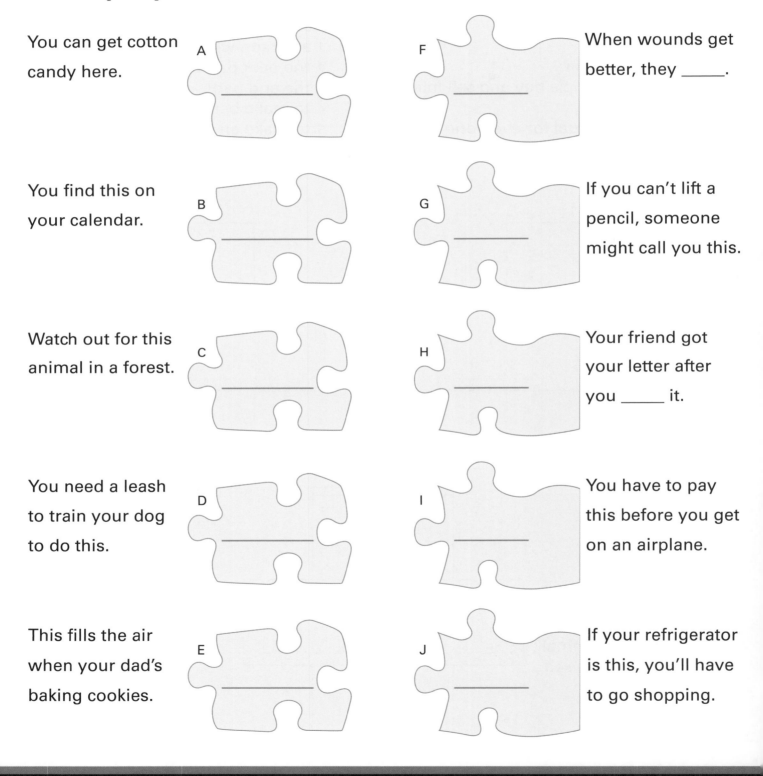

You can get cotton candy here.

A _____

You find this on your calendar.

B _____

Watch out for this animal in a forest.

C _____

You need a leash to train your dog to do this.

D _____

This fills the air when your dad's baking cookies.

E _____

When wounds get better, they _____.

F _____

If you can't lift a pencil, someone might call you this.

G _____

Your friend got your letter after you _____ it.

H _____

You have to pay this before you get on an airplane.

I _____

If your refrigerator is this, you'll have to go shopping.

J _____

Criss Cross

FILL IN the grid by answering the clues with keywords.

ACROSS

1. Not strong
2. The back of your foot
3. Hold up something heavy
4. Not stormy or cloudy
5. Perfume

DOWN

1. From Sunday to Saturday
2. To make healthy
3. Out in the open for all to see
4. Food
5. Shipped

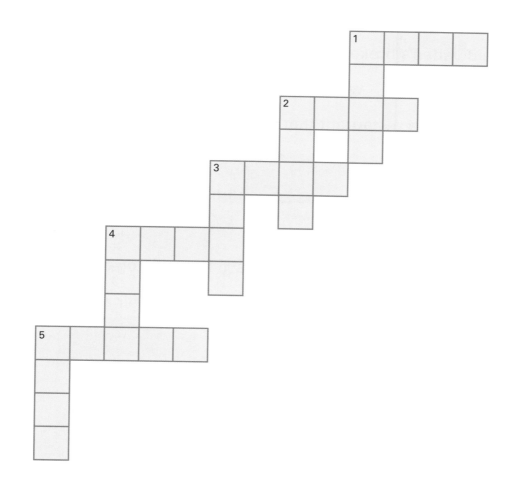

Blank Out!

FILL in the blanks with keywords.

bear	fare	heel	scent	weak
bare	fair	heal	sent	week

1. Jamie plans to sleep late every day during our _____ off from school.

2. It's _____ to take turns with your brother, but it's not always fun.

3. Kristen _____ a box full of toy spiders to her best friend.

4. Eric had to _____ his deepest secret to us during our game of Truth or Dare.

5. The doctors said Jaden's broken leg would take months to _____.

6. Jackson can't _____ waiting for the playoff game.

7. Mom wanted to eat at a restaurant that served French _____, but we just wanted pizza.

8. Everyone thought Trish was _____ until they watched her pick up the boy and lift him over her head.

9. Maya found out that it was impossible to teach her pet frog to _____.

10. Kevin still had the _____ of ocean water in his hair after he surfed all day.

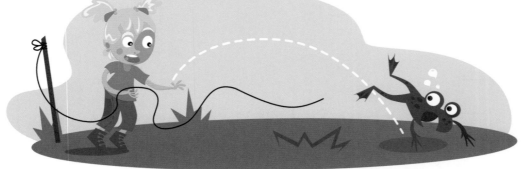

144

Double Trouble

CIRCLE the keyword that completes each sentence.

1. We should go to the park on the next fair / fare day.

2. Eli's new soccer cleats hurt his heel / heal.

3. Alexa will never throw away the stuffed bear / bare she got when she was a baby.

4. Hannah's favorite band is coming to town next weak / week.

5. Jenna loves everything about the circus, except for the sent / scent of the elephants.

6. Matt sometimes wishes his parents had sent / scent his sister to boarding school.

7. Tonya was still feeling week / weak from the flu.

8. Kim liked to ride her horse without a saddle, or bearback / bareback.

9. Our club wants to do things that will help heal / heel the Earth.

10. You can pay the fare / fair at the ticket counter.

Blank Out!

FILL in the blanks with keywords.

bear	fare	heel	scent	weak
bare	fair	heal	sent	week

1. This word describes a place where you'll find Ferris wheels and pig races.

   _____

2. This word tells what a restaurant serves. _____

3. This word describes seven days in a row on a calendar. _____

4. This word describes how you feel when you have no energy. _____

5. This word describes an animal that can catch fish in its sharp claws.

   _____

6. This word describes what you are in the shower. _____

7. This word tells what dogs use to sniff out clues. _____

8. When you talked back, your dad _____ you to your room.

9. This word describes the end of a loaf of bread. _____

10. This word tells how broken bones get better. They _____ .

 **Check It!**

Cut out the Check It! section on page 139, and see if you got the answers right.

Keywords

con•tent¹—kuhn-TEHNT *adjective* satisfied with what you have

con•tent²—KAHN-tehnt *noun* 1. the amount of something inside something else 2. the subject or topic covered 3. the meaning or truth of a creative work

con•tract¹—KAHN-trakt *noun* a legal agreement between two or more people or groups

con•tract²—kuhn-TRAKT *verb* 1. to draw or squeeze together 2. to shorten or make smaller

des•ert¹—DEHZ-ert *noun* a land that is dry and has few plants

de•sert²—dih-ZERT *verb* 1. to go away from 2. to leave someone that you should stay with 3. to quit and leave without permission

ob•ject¹—AHB-jehkt *noun* 1. something that you can see and touch 2. something that is the target of your thoughts or feelings 3. the reason for doing something

ob•ject²—ahb-JEHKT *verb* to go against or oppose with firm words

pres•ent¹—PREHZ-uhnt *noun* 1. something that is given to another 2. time that is happening now

pre•sent²—prih-ZEHNT *verb* 1. to introduce, to bring out before a group of people 2. to give

✓ Check It!

Page 148

Read & Replace

1. desert
2. object
3. content
4. present
5. content
6. object
7. desert
8. present
9. contract

Page 149

Homophone Hopscotch

1. desert
2. object
3. content

Page 150

Blank Out!

1. ob ject
2. con tent
3. pre sent
4. con tract
5. des ert

Page 151

Criss Cross

ACROSS	DOWN
2. contract	1. present
5. content	3. object
	4. desert

Double Trouble

1. tear
2. wind
3. bass
4. dove
5. pen
6. fan

✓ Check It!

Page 152

Blank Out!

1. contract
2. desert
3. object
4. present
5. content
6. desert
7. content
8. present
9. object
10. contract

Page 153

Double Match Up

1. f, m
2. b, l
3. c, n
4. e, o
5. h, p
6. i, t
7. j, s
8. k, q
9. d, r
10. a, g

Page 154

Blank Out!

1. content
2. desert
3. present
4. content
5. present
6. object
7. contract
8. desert
9. contract
10. object

Read & Replace

HOMOGRAPHS are words that have the same spelling but different meanings and sometimes different pronunciations. The *bill* of a duck and the *bill* that you pay are homographs. READ the story. FILL IN the blanks with keywords.

HINT: Read the whole story before you choose your words. Remember, each word has two meanings, so you can use it more than once.

| content | contract | desert | object | present |

"Let's go to the 1_____," Will shouted to his friends.

"I 2_____," said Stacey. "It's too hot today. I'm

3_____ to sit in the shade all day."

"Wait until you see the 4_____ I have," said Will.

Stacey took a piece of paper out of the box. "There are some

directions here, but I don't understand the 5_____."

It was a treasure map.

"There's an 6_____ buried under that X," Will

explained. "So are you coming, or are you going to

7_____ us?"

Stacey agreed to go, but first she scribbled something on a

piece of paper. She stopped to 8_____ the paper to

Will. "What's this?" asked Will.

"It's a 9_____," Stacey said. "It says that if we don't

find that treasure, you owe me a day in the shade."

Will shook Stacey's hand. "That's a deal—now let's go!"

Homograph Hopscotch

LOOK AT the definitions in each hopscotch board. FILL IN the matching keyword at the top of the board.

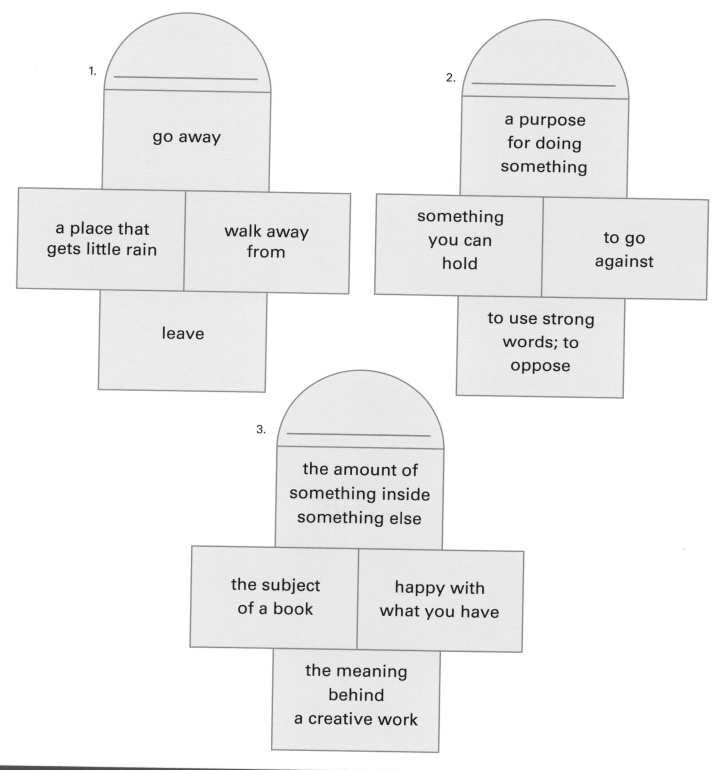

1. _____

go away

a place that gets little rain

walk away from

leave

2. _____

a purpose for doing something

something you can hold

to go against

to use strong words; to oppose

3. _____

the amount of something inside something else

the subject of a book

happy with what you have

the meaning behind a creative work

Blank Out!

FILL in the blanks with keywords. Then CIRCLE the syllable you say the strongest.

content	contract	desert	object	present

1. Kelly made a sculpture out of an _____ she found on the shore.

2. Tim's dog is _____ just chewing on an old bone.

3. The coach will _____ a golden basketball to T.J. at the awards dinner.

4. Jessica had to sign a _____ when she entered the video game competition.

5. Lizards and tortoises live in the _____.

Criss Cross

FILL IN the grid by answering the clues with keywords.

ACROSS

2. A legal agreement OR to make smaller

5. Satisfied OR the material in a book

DOWN

1. A gift OR to show something

3. To go against OR an item or thing

4. To leave OR a dry place

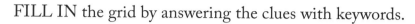

Double Trouble

WRITE the homograph that matches each description.

bass	dove	fan	pen	tear	wind

1. Water that comes from your eyes OR the way you rip paper _____

2. Moving air OR the way you spin around something else _____

3. A type of fish OR a low singer _____

4. A type of bird OR the way you went into the pool _____

5. Something you use to write OR a home for a pig _____

6. A person who loves a sport OR something that keeps you cool when you're hot _____

Blank Out!

FILL IN the blanks with keywords.

content	contract	desert	object	present

1. Jake and Caitlin signed a _____ before they started their babysitting business.

2. You should bring a bottle of water if you hike in the _____ .

3. Sarah is the _____ of Baxter's affection.

4. Thea and Joe will _____ their ideas to the band at practice.

5. We should take this thermos camping. It has a _____ of 2 liters.

6. We saw all the kids _____ the playground as soon as the storm started.

7. Carlos would be _____ to ride his dirt bike all day long.

8. We should make a _____ to give to Mom on Mother's Day.

9. No one will _____ if you want to wear your pink boots today.

10. I got a shot before my trip to Africa so I wouldn't _____ a strange disease.

Double Match Up

FIND the two meanings for each word. Then WRITE the letters of the definitions that match the word.

HINT: If you get stumped, use a dictionary or thesaurus.

1. arms _____ _____

2. hatch _____ _____

3. hide _____ _____

4. jam _____ _____

5. kind _____ _____

6. last _____ _____

7. sage _____ _____

8. story _____ _____

9. tap _____ _____

10. wake _____ _____

a. to stop sleeping
b. to come out of an egg
c. to keep out of sight
d. to strike lightly
e. a fruit spread
f. weapons
g. the track left by a moving ship
h. good-hearted
i. at the end
j. an herb
k. a tale

l. the opening in a ship's deck
m. the body parts between the shoulder and wrist
n. an animal skin
o. a difficult situation
p. a group with common traits
q. one floor level of a building
r. a faucet
s. a wise person
t. to keep going

Blank Out!

FILL IN the blanks with keywords.

content	contract	desert	object	present

1. This word describes how you feel if you open all your birthday presents and you've gotten everything you asked for. _____

2. If you leave your friend at the dance, you _____ her.

3. This word tells what you do when you show your trophy to your friends. You _____ it.

4. My mom won't let me see that movie. It has adult _____ .

5. This word tells what you cover with wrapping paper. _____

6. The _____ of basketball is to get the ball through the hoop.

7. This word tells what you might have to sign when you start a new after-school job. _____

8. This word describes a place where you hardly ever need an umbrella. _____

9. When you let air out of balloons, they _____ .

10. You might _____ if someone accuses you of lying when you told the truth.

 **Check It!**

Cut out Check It! to see if you got the answers right.

Just Right!

You've learned a lot of words so far. Are you ready to have some fun with them?

Synonyms may have similar meanings, but it's important to know which one is the right one to use in different situations. READ each sentence. Then CIRCLE the synonym that best fits the sentence.

1. Greg will need a needle and thread to mend , repair his torn shirt.

2. The mechanic can mend , repair our car.

3. Dad is afraid our old garden hose will fracture , rupture.

4. Victor might fracture , rupture his arm if he tries that trick again.

5. We had to help mom locate , discover her missing keys.

6. Brian was sure he could locate , discover a new species of insect.

7. You can improve , recover your skating by practicing.

8. We have a enough , sufficient amount of food for the picnic.

9. Sal is trying to acquire , gain a computer for the afterschool club.

10. Kelly might advance , approach you to ask for a favor.

11. The coaches will give , provide all of our equipment.

12. They manufacture , invent action figures in that factory.

13. Raina is waiting for you to react , respond to her invitation.

14. Tito will inquire , request about the movie times on Saturday.

15. Nina liked the original , unique version of the song better than the new one.

✓ Check It!

Page 155

Just Right!

1. mend
2. repair
3. rupture
4. fracture
5. locate
6. discover
7. improve
8. sufficient
9. acquire
10. approach
11. provide
12. manufacture
13. respond
14. inquire
15. original

Page 156

Pathfinder

1. enormous, tiny
2. gloomy, bright
3. gradual, rapid
4. humorous, serious
5. minuscule, colossal
6. vanish, appear

Page 157

Fixer Upper

1. bear
2. fare
3. heal
4. scent
5. weak

Double Trouble

1. content: satisfied with what you have
2. contract: a legal agreement
3. desert: to go away from
4. object: something you can see and touch
5. present: a gift

Pathfinder

Antonyms are opposites, and knowing your opposites can get you a long way in this game. Begin at START. When you get to a box with two arrows, follow the antonym to a new word. If you make all the right choices, you'll end up at FINISH.

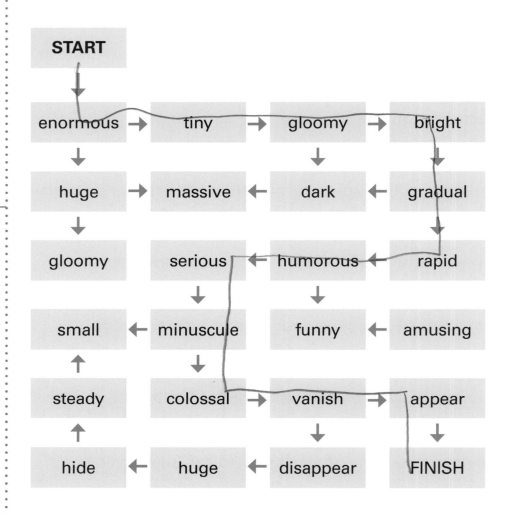

Fixer Upper

Our homophones have gotten all mixed up. READ the glossary. REPLACE each keyword with the homophone that matches the definition.

bare	1. a large animal in the mammal family	_____
fair	2. the money you pay when you get on a bus	_____
heel	3. to make healthy	_____
sent	4. a smell	_____
week	5. not strong	_____

Double Trouble

Write another meaning for each keyword.

content	1. the subject covered OR _____
contract	2. to make smaller OR _____
desert	3. a dry land OR _____
object	4. to go against OR _____
present	5. to introduce OR _____

Sniglets!

English is always growing and changing. Every year, hundreds of new words are added to the dictionary.

Sniglets are fun-sounding words, but they haven't quite made it to the dictionary yet. Here are some sniglets:

purrsuasion—when a cat rubs up against you trying to get some food
eggsactly—eggs that are cooked just the way you like them
rowedblock—what happens when you're too tired to row your boat any further
starecase—a person who won't stop staring at you
whethervane—a device you spin to tell whether or not you should do something
younicycle—your bicycle

WRITE a sniglet from the list to complete each sentence.

1. We were almost across the lake when Michael got _____.

2. Did you ride your _____ to school?

3. They're going to let the _____ decide which movie they'll go to.

4. Dad cooked _____ and bacon for breakfast.

5. Whiskers thinks she can use _____ to get dinner.

6. Mom can be such a _____ when she's angry.

Now it's your turn. Here are some homophones that might inspire a sniglet or two.

ate/eight	dew/do/due	hare/hair	meat/meet
pause/paws	peace/piece	pedal/peddle/petal	which/witch
tail/tale	right/rite/write		

_____

_____

_____

✓ Check It!

Cut out Check It! to see if you got the answers right.

Keywords

pre•cau•tion—prih-KAW-shun *noun* something done beforehand to prevent harm

pre•his•tor•ic—pree-hih-STAWR-ihk *adjective* relating to something that happened before written history

pre•school—PREE-skool *noun* the school a child attends before elementary school

pre•view—PREE-vyoo *verb* to show or look at in advance

re•ar•range—ree-uh-RAYNJ *verb* to put things in a new order or position

re•play—ree-PLAY *verb* to play again

re•view—rih-VYOO *verb* 1. to look at again 2. to report on the quality of something 3. to study or check again

sub•ma•rine—suhb-muh-REEN *noun* a vehicle that operates underwater

sub•top•ic—SUHB-tahp-ihk *noun* a topic that is a part of the main topic

sub•way—SUHB-way *noun* 1. a passage underneath the ground 2. an underground railway

✓ Check It!

Page 160

Read & Replace

1. preschool
2. preview
3. prehistoric
4. submarine
5. review
6. precaution
7. rearrange
8 replay
9. subway
10. subtopic

Page 161

Petal Power

1. pre
2. sub
3. re
4. pre
5. sub
6. re

Page 162

Tic-Tac-Toe

1. topic, way, group
2. historic, normal, school
3. soil, marine, topic

subtopic	precook
subway	pregame
submarine	preview
subtitle	prehistoric
subgroup	prejudge
remake	
recall	
review	
recheck	

Prefixes

✓ Check It!

Page 163

Criss Cross

ACROSS
2. review
3. prehistoric
5. precaution
6. subway

DOWN
1. preschool
4. replay

Page 164

Blank Out!

1. submarine
2. prehistoric
3. review
4. rearrange
5. subway
6. preview
7. replay
8. preschool
9. subtopic
10. precaution

Page 165

It's Puzzling!

1. predawn
2. preexist
3. preoccupied
4. reappear
5. recount
6. refresh
7. subplot
8. subterranean

Page 166

Blank Out!

1. preschool
2. subway
3. submarine
4. rearrange
5. precaution
6. subtopic
7. review
8. preview
9. replay
10. prehistoric

Read & Replace

PREFIXES are groups of letters that come at the beginning of a word. Each prefix has its own meaning. READ the story. FILL IN the blanks with keywords.

Prefix Meanings: pre = before   sub = under   re = again

One day, Tammy visited her little brother in 1_____.

She thought his class just played all day, so they could get

a 2_____ of elementary school. But her brother's friend

Adam knew all about 3_____ creatures like dinosaurs. A

girl named Casey played with the toy 4_____ at the water

table to see what floated and what sank. When the teacher did a

5_____ of fire safety, Tammy even learned a 6_____

she should take in a fire: Get low and go! Tammy helped the kids

7_____ the furniture in the housekeeping center. She

played Duck, Duck, Goose with her brother's friends, but she got

a little tired on the twentieth 8_____ of the game. Tammy

and her brother took the 9_____ home. "I learned a lot

from you today, little brother," she said. "I think you've even

given me an idea

for a 10_____

for my report on games

children play."

Petal Power

READ the words around each flower. Then WRITE a prefix that could be added to each root word in the flower to make another word.

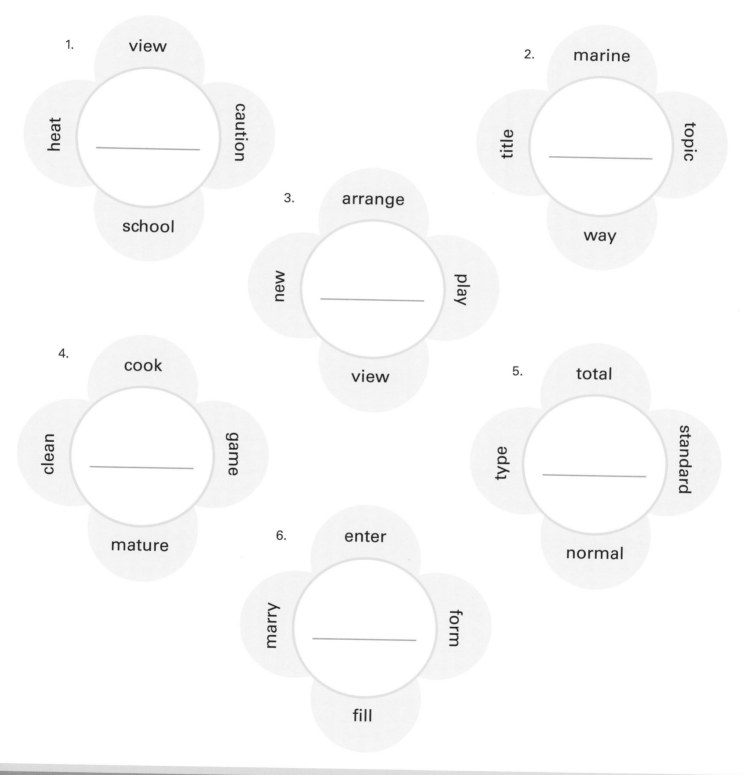

1. view
   heat
   caution
   school

2. marine
   title
   topic
   way

3. arrange
   new
   play
   view

4. cook
   clean
   game
   mature

5. total
   type
   standard
   normal

6. enter
   marry
   form
   fill

Prefixes

Tic-Tac-Toe

PLAY Tic-tac-toe with prefixes. CIRCLE any root that could be used with the prefix in blue. PUT an X through any word that could not be used with the prefix. When you find three X's or O's in a row, you're a winner! The line can go across, down, or diagonally. When you're done, make a list of all the words.

1. sub

view	topic	caution
cycle	way	marine
title	group	fix

2. re

make	topic	historic
call	view	normal
way	check	school

3. pre

soil	cook	game
way	marine	view
historic	judge	topic

Other Words Created with Prefixes

_____

_____

_____

_____

_____

Criss Cross

FILL IN the grid by answering the clues with keywords.

ACROSS

2. What you do when you look back over your notes to get ready for a test

3. Cavemen lived in these times

5. Wearing a helmet when you skate is a ____

6. A train line that runs underground

DOWN

1. The school where you go before kindergarten

4. What you do when you play a song again

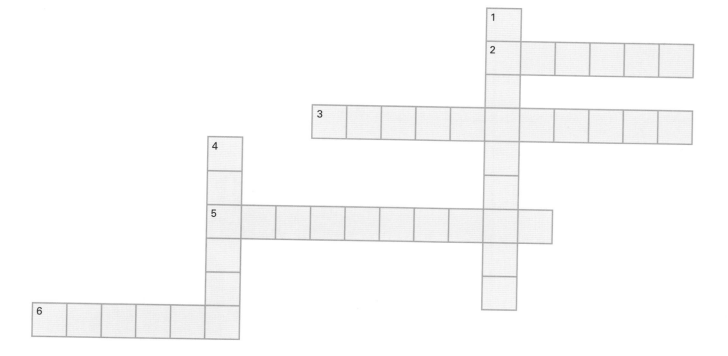

Prefixes

Blank Out!

FILL IN the blanks with keywords.

| precaution | prehistoric | preschool | preview | rearrange |
| replay | review | submarine | subtopic | subway |

1. Jason could see an octopus out of the window of the _____.

2. A wooly mammoth is a creature from _____ times.

3. Henry will _____ the play for the school newspaper.

4. We can _____ our desks for April Fool's Day.

5. Francesco was afraid to ride the _____ alone.

6. Tito looked for a _____ of the new video game online.

7. The referee told the football team they had to _____ a down because of the penalty.

8. Maria liked to finger-paint when she was in _____.

9. "Moto-cross" is a _____ in Mark's report about extreme sports.

10. Keira uses sunblock as a _____ when she goes sailing.

It's Puzzling!

MATCH each prefix to a root word. Then WRITE the words in the blanks.

HINT: You can use the same prefix more than once.

pre-

re-

sub-

terranean

occupied

appear

dawn

plot

fresh

count

exist

Blank Out!

FILL IN the blanks with keywords.

precaution	prehistoric	preschool	preview	rearrange
replay	review	submarine	subtopic	subway

1. Before kindergarten, you went to _____.

2. To travel under the ground you can use a _____.

3. People explore under the sea in a _____.

4. You _____ your room to change the way it looks.

5. Before a big storm hits, you buy supplies as a _____.

6. The section titled "Fantasy Games" in your gamer guide is a _____.

7. Before buying the newest game, be sure to read a _____ of it.

8. A _____ shows a clip of a movie that's coming soon.

9. If you want to watch a DVD movie again after it's over, you _____ it.

10. T. Rex stamped around in _____ times.

6

Keywords

dis•hon•est—dihs-AHN-ihst *adjective* lying, not honest

dis•please—dihs-PLEEZ *verb* to make someone feel dislike or annoyance

dis•sim•i•lar—dih-SIHM-uh-ler *adjective* different, unlike

non•mov•ing—nahn-MOO-vihng *adjective* in a fixed position, not changing place or position

non•sense—NAHN-sehns *noun* silly or meaningless words or actions

non•tox•ic—nahn-TAHK-sihk *adjective* not poisonous, harmless

un•com•fort•a•ble—uhn-CUHM-fert-uh-buhl *adjective* not feeling or giving comfort

un•like•ly—uhn-LIK-lee *adjective* not likely to happen

un•u•su•al—uhn-YOO-zhoo-uhl *adjective* not common, rare

un•wise—uhn-WIZ *adjective* not wise, foolish

✓ Check It!

Page 168
Read & Replace

1. uncomfortable
2. nonsense
3. dishonest
4. unwise
5. displease
6. unlikely
7. dissimilar
8. nontoxic
9. nonmoving

Page 169
Petal Power

1. dis
2. non
3. un
4. dis
5. non
6. un

Page 170
Tic-Tac-Toe

1. sense, skid, stop
2. certain, button, easy
3. fiction, cling, final

nonsense	uncertain	disappoint
nonskid	unbutton	dislike
nonstop	uneasy	disloyal
nondairy	uncut	disgrace
	undo	distrust

Page 171
Criss Cross

ACROSS
3. uncomfortable
4. unlikely
6. nontoxic
7. dissimilar
8. unusual

DOWN
1. unwise
2. nonmoving
5. nonsense

Read & Replace

The prefixes *dis*, *non*, and *un* share the same meaning: *not*. These prefixes at the beginning of a word tell you that the word means the opposite of the root word. *Unwise* is the opposite of *wise*.

READ the story. FILL IN the blanks with keywords.

dishonest	displease	dissimilar
nonmoving	nonsense	nontoxic
uncomfortable	unlikely	unwise

Ned was starting to wonder about his friend Paul. Paul told

stories, and some of them made Ned feel 1_____.

Sometimes the stories were so wild they just seemed

like 2_____—like the time Paul said that he had seen an

creature with a head like a horse and a body like a tiger. Ned

didn't like to think that his friend was being 3_____, but

he knew it was 4_____ for Paul to tell these stories.

Ned didn't want to 5_____ his friend, but he knew it

was 6_____that Paul would change unless someone

talked to him. Ned always thought his best friend was just like

him, but now he felt like he and Paul were 7_____.

So when Paul told all their friends that he was going to drink

rattlesnake venom and survive, Ned said, "Paul, that's pineapple

juice. You know it's 8_____." Paul just stared, like

a 9_____ object, but later he told Ned that he had never

had a better friend.

Petal Power

READ the words around each flower. Then WRITE a prefix that could be added to each root word in the flower to make another word.

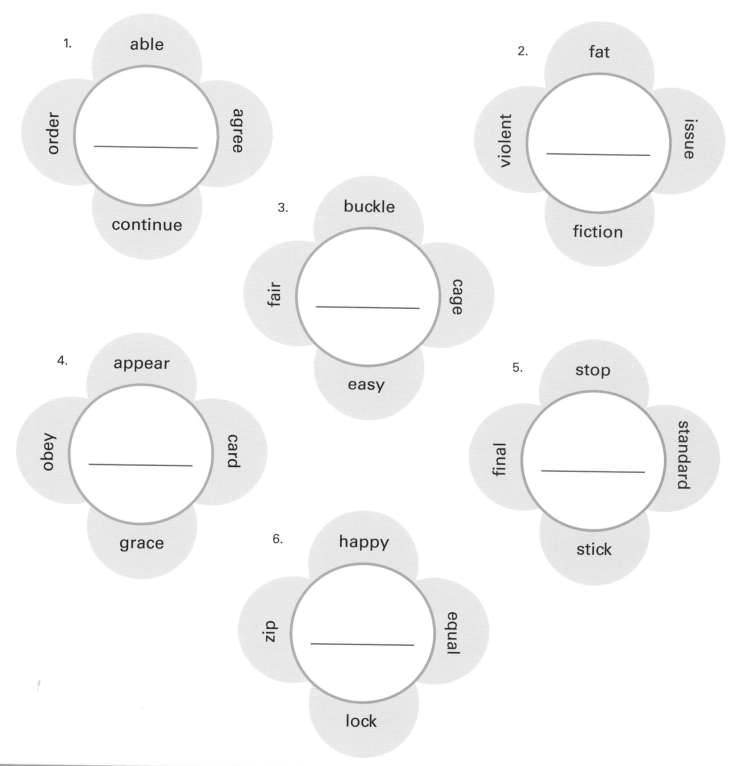

1. able
order
agree
_____
continue

2. fat
violent
issue
_____
fiction

3. buckle
fair
cage
_____
easy

4. appear
obey
card
_____
grace

5. stop
final
standard
_____
stick

6. happy
zip
equal
_____
lock

Tic-Tac-Toe

PLAY Tic-tac-toe with prefixes. CIRCLE any root word that could be used with the prefix in blue. PUT an X through any word that could not be used with the prefix. When you find three X's or O's in a row, you are a winner! The line can go across, down, or diagonally. When you're done, make a list of all the words.

1. non

cling	sense	wind
cover	skid	dairy
fair	stop	fit

2. un

certain	place	stop
button	toxic	cut
easy	do	respect

3. dis

fiction	appoint	like
even	cling	loyal
grace	trust	final

Other Words Created with Prefixes

_____

_____

_____

_____

_____

Criss Cross

FILL IN the grid by answering the clues with keywords.

ACROSS

3. The opposite of comfortable
4. The opposite of likely
6. The opposite of toxic
7. The opposite of similar
8. The opposite of usual

DOWN

1. The opposite of wise
2. The opposite of moving
5. The opposite of sense

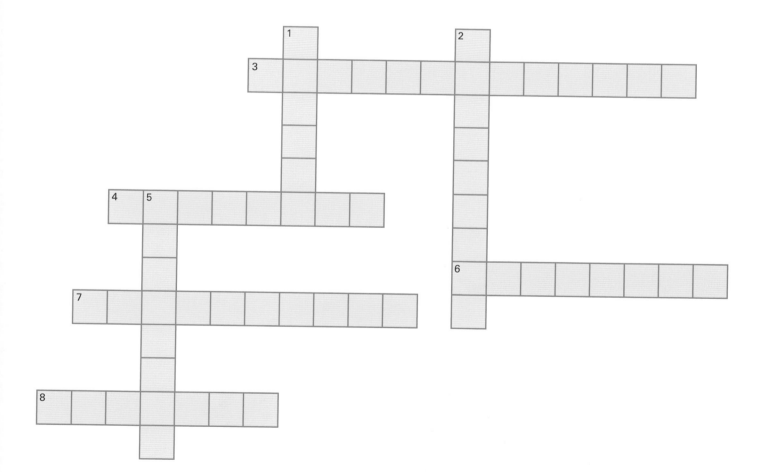

Blank Out!

FILL IN the blanks with keywords.

1. It is _____ that your grandmother rides a dirt bike.

2. A rock would make an _____ pillow.

3. A slide is a _____ object at the playground.

4. Tom likes soccer and his brother likes gymnastics. They are _____.

5. It's a good thing crayons are _____, as my baby sister eats them all the time.

6. It would _____ your friend if you said mean things about her.

7. Lisa was being _____. She said she didn't eat the cookies, but she did.

8. It is _____ to swim during a thunderstorm.

9. A hedgehog is an _____ pet.

10. It's hard to understand someone who is speaking _____.

It's Puzzling!

MATCH each prefix to a root word. Then WRITE the words in the blanks.

HINT: You can use the same prefix more than once.

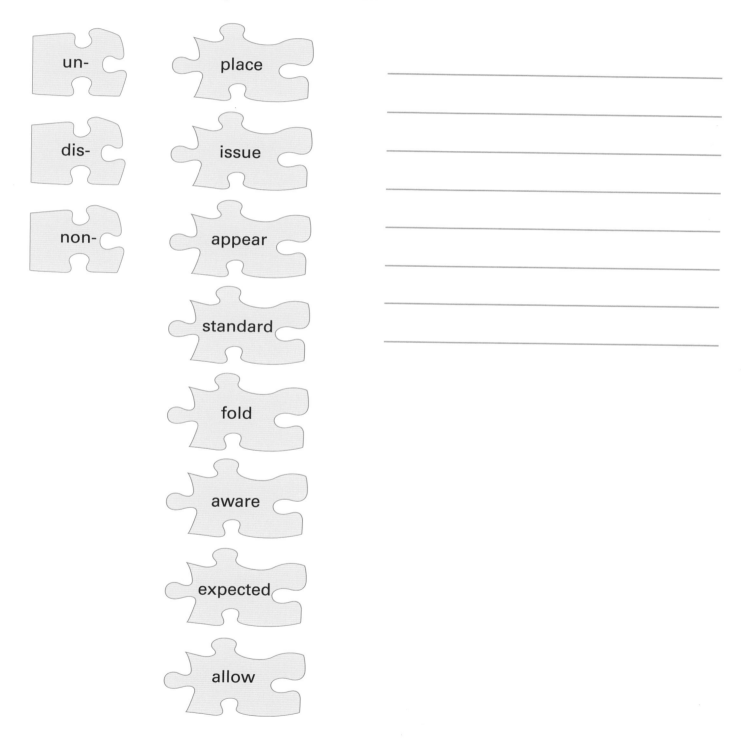

un-

dis-

non-

place

issue

appear

standard

fold

aware

expected

allow

_____

_____

_____

_____

_____

_____

_____

_____

Blank Out!

FILL IN the blanks with keywords.

1. The possibility of a snowstorm in a desert is _____.

2. Kids who say the dog ate their homework are usually _____.

3. My brother invented his own language. I think it sounds like _____.

4. To put on clothes you've outgrown can be _____.

5. The sizes of elephants and ants is _____.

6. When your friends make you unhappy, they _____ you.

7. Violet-colored eyes are _____.

8. Deciding to wear sandals in the snow is _____.

9. _____ chemicals won't harm you.

10. A car with an engine that doesn't work is _____.

Keywords

care•less—KAYR-lihs *adjective* 1. not paying careful attention to 2. done, made, or said without care

end•less—EHND-lihs *adjective* 1. without end or limits 2. joined at the ends

en•ter•tain•ment—en-ter-TAYN-muhnt *noun* ways to give pleasure to or amuse people, such as singing, dancing, and acting

fear•ful—FEER-fuhl *adjective* 1. filled with fear 2. nervous and easily frightened

grate•ful—GRAYT-fuhl *adjective* having the desire to thank someone

move•ment—MOOV-muhnt *noun* 1. the act of changing location or position 2. the way in which somebody or something moves

pain•less—PAYN-lihs *adjective* 1. not causing pain 2. involving little difficulty

play•ful—PLAY-fuhl *adjective* 1. full of play, fond of playing 2. said or done in a fun way

pun•ish•ment—PUHN-ihsh-muhnt *noun* 1. the act of punishing 2. a penalty for wrongdoing 3. rough treatment

truth•ful—TROOTH-fuhl *adjective* honest, true, always telling the truth

---

✓ Check It!

Page 176
Read & Replace

1. truthful
2. fearful
3. playful
4. punishment
5. movement
6. careless
7. endless
8. grateful
9. entertainment
10. painless

Page 177
Suffix Hopscotch

1. ment
2. less
3. ful

Page 178
Match Up

1. -ment, d
2. -ful, e
3. -less, b
4. -less, f
5. -ful, c
6. -ment, a

Page 179
Criss Cross

ACROSS
1. playful
4. entertainment
6. grateful
7. movement

DOWN
1. painless
2. truthful
3. punishment
4. endless
5. careless

Read & Replace

A SUFFIX comes at the end of a word and has its own meaning. The suffix "-ful" at the end of the word *playful* means *full of*. READ the letter. FILL IN the blanks with keywords.

Dear Brian,

Yesterday, I went to see my sister Ava's play. I have to be

1_____ and say that it was terrible. I am 2_____

that you will come to see it. You would think a musical would

be 3_____. You would be wrong. The music was

4_____ on my ears. There were dancers, but there was

little 5_____. The costumes must have been sewn by a

6_____ designer. Some of them fell apart on the stage!

The first act went on for more than two hours. It seemed

7_____! I was 8_____ when the play actually

did end. They may call it 9_____, but I like my fun to be

10_____, and this was hard to sit through.

Sharon

P.S. Please don't tell Ava about this letter—I told her the play

was fantastic!

Suffix Hopscotch

LOOK AT the words in each hopscotch board. FILL IN a suffix that can be added to all of the words in the board.

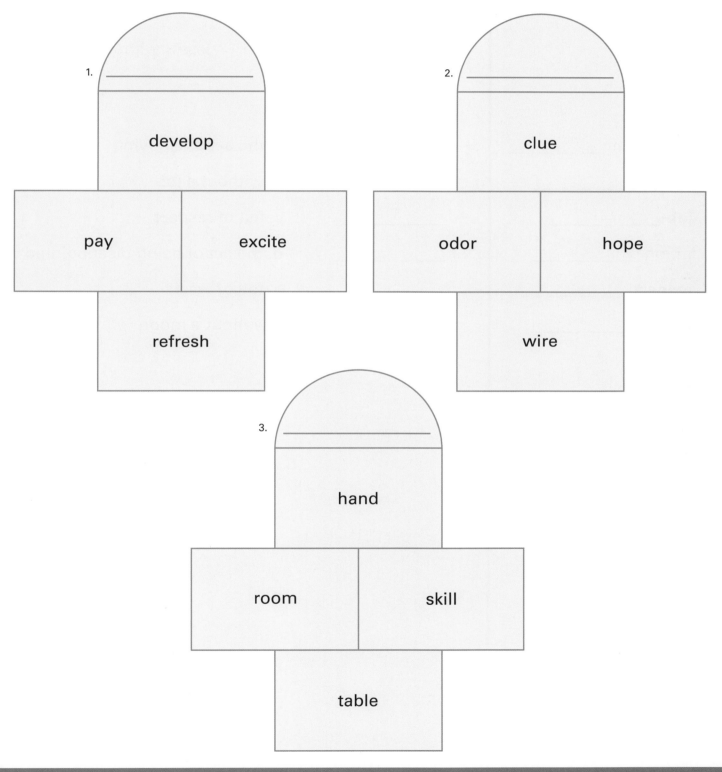

1. _____

develop

pay   excite

refresh

2. _____

clue

odor   hope

wire

3. _____

hand

room   skill

table

Match Up

MATCH each root word to its suffix and write the suffix in the blank. USE the suffix box to help you. Then MATCH a definition for each word by writing the letters in the blanks.

ful = full of	ment = act of	less = without

Definition

1. disappoint _____   _____   a. the act of enjoying

2. waste _____   _____   b. without a job

3. job _____   _____   c. full of respect

4. moon _____   _____   d. the act of being disappointed

5. respect _____   _____   e. full of waste

6. enjoy _____   _____   f. without a moon

Criss Cross

FILL IN the grid by answering the clues with keywords.

ACROSS

1. Fond of playing
4. Singing, dancing, acting
6. Full of thanks
7. The act of moving

DOWN

1. Without pain
2. Telling the truth
3. Rough treatment
4. Having no end
5. Something done without care

Blank Out!

FILL IN the blanks with keywords.

careless ✓ ✓	endless	entertainment ✓	fearful	grateful
movement ✓	painless ✓	playful	punishment	truthful ✓

1. Katie knew she could not be _____ if she wanted to land the 360 on her skateboard.

2. Scary movies are his favorite form of ~~_____~~ entertainment.

3. Lee had to clean the garage as his _____ for not doing his chores.

4. The ocean looks _____ when you're standing on the shore.

5. Puppies are always running and jumping. They are very _____ creatures.

6. If you are _Careless_ when you eat pizza, you could end up with a shirt full of sauce.

7. The doctor said the shot would be _painless_, but it did hurt a little.

8. Yolanda liked to sit on the roof of her building and watch the _movement_ of the crowd below.

9. Dad said Jared won't get punished if he is _truhful_ about what happened.

10. Briana is _____ for the inventor of the jelly bean. It's her favorite snack!

I ♥ Jelly beans

It's Puzzling!

MATCH each suffix to a root word. Then WRITE the words in the blanks.

HINT: You can use the same suffix more than once.

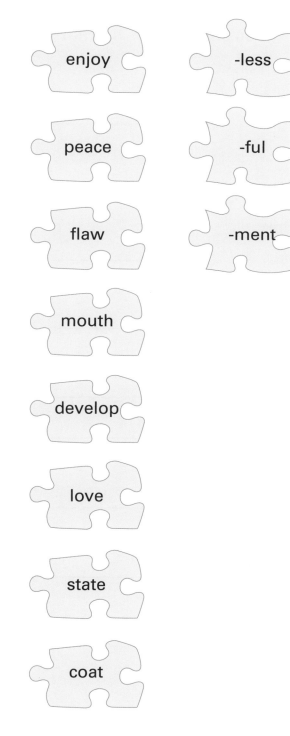

enjoy

peace

flaw

mouth

develop

love

state

coat

-less

-ful

-ment

_____

_____

_____

_____

_____

_____

_____

Blank Out!

FILL IN the blanks with keywords.

careless	endless	entertainment	fearful	grateful
movement	painless	playful	punishment	truthful

1. This word is another word for popular books, movies, and music.

   _____

2. This word describes how you feel when someone does something nice for you.

   _____

3. This word tells what you might get if you don't follow your parents' rules.

   _____

4. This word describes the way you wish every visit to the dentist will be.

   _____

5. This word describes how you might feel face to face with a great white shark.

   _____

6. This word describes the universe.

   _____

7. This word describes what you might have been if you knocked over a bottle of juice.

   _____

8. This word tells what you should be if you want people to believe you.

   _____

9. This word describes what you can see if you watch a butterfly's wings as it flies.

   _____

10. This word tells how you might feel when you're at the park with your friends.

    _____

Keywords

bright•ly—BRIT-lee *adverb* 1. in a way that gives off a lot of light 2. in a way that seems happy and cheerful

damp•ness—DAMP-nuhs *noun* the quality of being slightly wet

feath•er•y—FEH*TH*-uh-ree *adjective* 1. like a feather 2. covered in feathers

fi•nal•ly—FIN-uhl-ee *adverb* 1. after a long period of time 2. happening at the end or last

loud•ness—LOWD-nuhs *noun* 1. the degree of volume of sound

re•cent•ly—REES-uhnt-lee *adverb* relating to a time not long ago

shad•ow•y—SHAD-oh-ee *adjective* 1. full of shadows 2. not clearly seen 3. not realistic

sly•ness—SLI-nuhs *noun* the quality of being sneaky or smart at hiding one's goals

sneak•y—SNEE-kee *adjective* doing things in a secret and sometimes unfair way

speed•i•ly—SPEED-uhl-ee *adverb* with quickness

Check It!

Page 184

Read & Replace

1. recently
2. shadowy
3. feathery
4. slyness
5. sneaky
6. dampness
7. finally
8. brightly
9. loudness
10. speedily

Page 185

Suffix Hopscotch

1. ness
2. y
3. ly

Page 186

Match Up

1. buttery: like butter
2. deafness: the state of being deaf
3. wisely: in the manner of one who is wise
4. fitness: the state of being fit
5. totally: relating to the total
6. rainy: wet with rain

Page 187

Criss Cross

ACROSS	DOWN
2. brightly	1. finally
3. dampness	4. sneaky
6. recently	5. loudness
8. slyness	7. feathery
10. speedily	9. shadowy

Read & Replace

READ the field notes. FILL IN the blanks with keywords.

brightly	dampness	feathery	finally	loudness
recently	shadowy	slyness	sneaky	speedily

Field Notes

1_____ I made a most amazing discovery. I was

exploring the 2_____ depths of a remote rainforest

when I saw a creature dash through the leaves. All I could see

was its 3_____ tail. I had never seen a tail quite like

it before. I wanted to catch the creature so I could observe it

more closely. I was sure my partner and I could use our

4_____ to trick the creature. We created a 5_____

plan. We believed that the creature liked the 6_____ of

the rainforest floor. We covered our bodies with moss and

spread out on the ground. We were thrilled when we

7_____ saw the creature's 8_____ colored

feathers. We quickly grabbed it in our hands. Unfortunately the

9_____ of the creature's call shocked us.

It sounded just like a fog horn! My partner

and I grabbed our ears, and when

we did, the creature

10_____ escaped

from our hands.

Suffix Hopscotch

LOOK AT the root words in each hopscotch board. FILL IN a suffix that can be added to all of the words in the board.

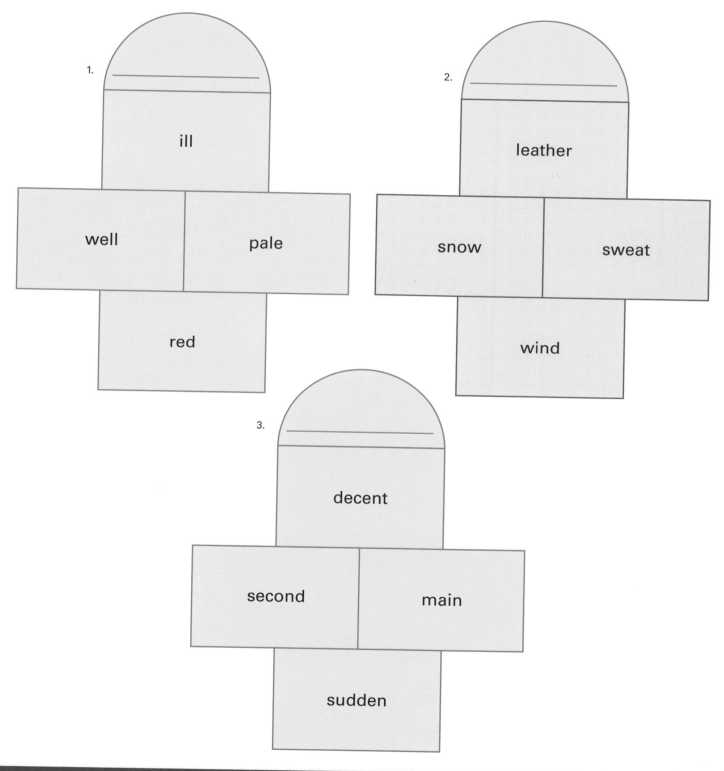

1. _____

ill

well   pale

red

2. _____

leather

snow   sweat

wind

3. _____

decent

second   main

sudden

Match Up

MATCH each word to a suffix. Then USE the suffix box to help you WRITE a definition for each word.

-ly = in the manner of; relating to

-ness = state of

-y = state, condition, or result of

	Root	Suffix	Word
1.	butter	ly	_____
2.	deaf	y	_____
3.	wise	ness	_____
4.	fit	ly	_____
5.	total	y	_____
6.	rain	ness	_____

Definitions

1. _____

2. _____

3. _____

4. _____

5. _____

6. _____

Criss Cross

FILL IN the grid by answering the clues with keywords.

ACROSS

2. In a cheerful manner
3. The state of being slightly wet
6. Happening not long ago
8. The quality of being smart at hiding one's motives
10. With quickness

DOWN

1. At last
4. In a secret way
5. The degree of volume of a sound
7. Like a feather
9. Resembling a shadow

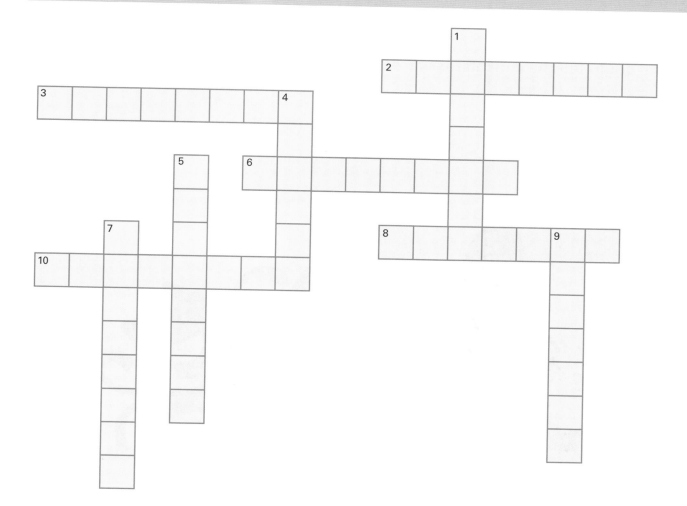

Blank Out!

FILL IN the blanks with keywords.

1. The full moon _____ lights up the sky.

2. Valerie is making _____ wings for her costume.

3. The team was excited to hear the _____ of the crowd.

4. It's always sad when summer is _____ over.

5. Martin used his _____ to play an April Fool's prank on his best friend.

6. Carol rode her bike _____ down the hill.

7. The _____ of the basement gave Anna a chill.

8. Paul's cat was being _____ when it crept up on my dog.

9. Brynn could tell the chocolates were not bought _____.

   They tasted stale.

10. Billy was scared to walk in the _____ forest.

It's Puzzling!

MATCH each suffix to a root word. Then WRITE the words in the blanks.

HINT: You can use the same suffix more than once.

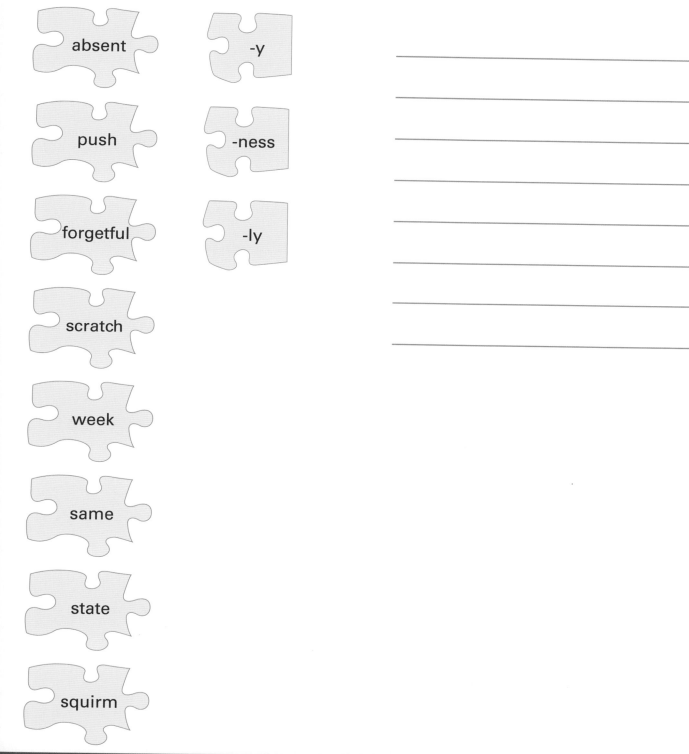

absent

-y

push

-ness

forgetful

-ly

scratch

week

same

state

squirm

Blank Out!

FILL IN the blanks with keywords.

1. This word describes most birds. _____

2. This word tells what an alley looks like at night. _____

3. This word tells when you ate breakfast if you just finished it an hour ago.

   _____

4. This word describes the way you act when you play a trick on your sister.

   _____

5. This word tells about the moisture in the air on a cold morning. _____

6. This word tells what fills a room when you shout out the words to your favorite

   song. _____

7. This word tells how you'd want to run in a race. _____

8. This word tells when the package you've been waiting for actually arrives.

   _____

9. This word tells what you need to use to find out a secret your best friend doesn't

   want to tell you. _____

10. This word describes how you might smile when you find out you're going

    somewhere great on vacation. _____

Pick the One!

Think you've got your prefixes straight? It's time to check your skills. LOOK AT each group of words. CIRCLE the actual English word in each row.

1.	premarine	nonmarine	submarine
2.	discaution	precaution	uncaution
3.	replay	subplay	unplay
4.	preschool	reschool	subschool
5.	nonsense	subsense	unsense
6.	disway	unway	subway
7.	recomfortable	subcomfortable	uncomfortable
8.	prelikely	relikely	unlikely
9.	subplease	displease	unpleased
10.	rehonest	prehonest	dishonest

Combo Mambo

WRITE all the words you can make by adding the prefixes to the root words.

dis-	non-	pre-	re-	sub-	un-

1. view _____

2. play _____

3. arrange _____

4. moving _____

✓ Check It!

Page 191

Pick the One!

1. submarine	6. subway
2. precaution	7. uncomfortable
3. replay	8. unlikely
4. preschool	9. displease
5. nonsense	10. dishonest

Combo Mambo

1. preview, review
2. display, replay
3. prearrange, rearrange
4. removing, nonmoving, unmoving

Page 192

Pick the One!

1. finally	4. shadowy
2. dampness	5. sneaky
3. movement	6. playful

Combo Mambo

1. featherless, feathery
2. brightly, brightness
3. careful, careless
4. slyly, slyness
5. loudly, loudness
6. painful, painless

Page 193

Pathfinder

1. historic, pre
2. fear, ful
3. similar, dis
4. punish, ment
5. toxic, non
6. recent, ly

Page 194

Sniglets!

1. nonreturner	4. snackful
2. subscratch	5. wowless
3. unfriend	6. predreams

Suggestions:
1. monocatch—when you play catch with yourself
2. teletalk—when you have a conversation with someone who is across the room
3. videogamation—the act of playing a video game

Pick the One!

Now it's time to test your knowledge of suffixes. You know the rules—just CIRCLE the actual English words. Ready, set, go!

1. finalless   finalment   finally

2. dampful   dampness   dampy

3. moveless   movely   movement

4. shadowful   shadowness   shadowy

5. sneakly   sneaky   sneakful

6. playless   playly   playful

Combo Mambo

WRITE all the words you can make by adding the suffixes to the root words.

ful	less	ly	ment	ness	y

1. feather _____

2. bright _____

3. care _____

4. sly _____

5. loud _____

6. pain _____

Pathfinder

Think you know your prefixes and suffixes pretty well? Then you'll have no problem with this game. Begin at START. When you get to a box with two arrows, pick the prefix or suffix that you can add to the root word. If you make all the right choices, you'll end up at FINISH.

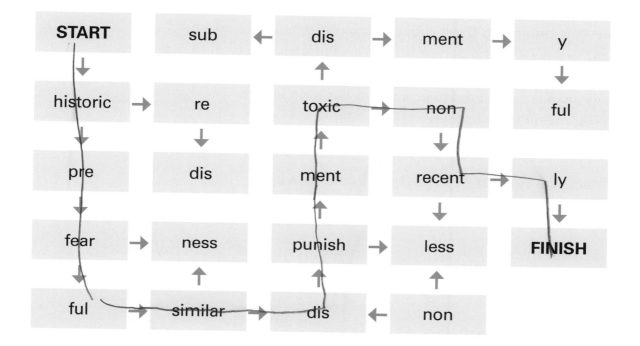

Sniglets!

Are you ready for some more sniglet fun? Remember, sniglets are fun-sounding words that haven't quite made it to the dictionary yet. Here are some sniglets made with the prefixes and suffixes you just reviewed.

snackful—when you've eaten so many snacks that you can't eat any more
predream—the things you think about before you actually fall asleep
nonreturner—a person who doesn't bring back library books until they're overdue
subscratch—the act of raking through the bottom of a backpack in search of a missing item
unfriend—someone who used to be a friend but is no longer
wowless—not thrilling or exciting

WRITE a singlet from the list to complete each sentence.

1. Violet had to pay a lot of fines because she was a _____.

2. Let me just _____ to see if I can find a piece of gum.

3. Sam became my _____ when he told Helen my secret.

4. We held our stomachs and groaned in pain because we were _____.

5. The concert was so _____ we left early.

6. I had so many _____ that I couldn't fall asleep.

Now it's your turn. Here are some prefixes and suffixes you can use to create more sniglets.

Prefixes	Suffixes
hyper- = over, above	-ation = action
mono- = one	-ize = cause
poly- = many	-ism = belief
tele- = distance	-ory = a place for

_____

_____

_____

_____

Keywords

au•di•ble—AW-duh-buhl *adjective* able to be heard

au•di•ence—AW-dee-uhns *noun* a group that listens or watches

au•di•o—AW-dee-oh *adjective* 1. relating to sound that can be heard 2. relating to the recording or reproduction of sound

au•di•tion—aw-DIHSH-uhn *noun* 1. the sense of hearing 2. a test performance by a musician, singer, dancer, or actor

au•di•to•ri•um—awd-ih-TAWR-ee-uhm *noun* a building, or the area of a building, where the audience sits

dic•tate—DIHK-tayt *verb* 1. to speak or read for someone to write down 2. to give orders or rule over

dic•ta•tor—DIHK-tay-ter *noun* a leader who rules with total power over others

dic•tion•ar•y—DIHK-shuh-nehr-ee *noun* a reference book that lists words in alphabetical order and explains their meanings

pre•dict—prih-DIHKT *verb* to tell what is going to happen in the future

ver•dict—VER-dihkt *noun* 1. the decision a jury reaches together 2. an opinion about something

✓ Check It!

Page 196
Read & Replace

1. auditorium
2. predict
3. audition
4. dictator
5. audio
6. audible
7. verdict
8. dictate
9. audience
10. dictionary

Page 197
Root It Out

1. dictator
2. auditorium
3. verdict
4. audible
5. dictionary
6. audio
7. predict
8. audience
9. dictate
10. audition

Page 198
Combo Mambo

1. audiovisual: relating to sound and vision
2. audit: to tell the details of
3. auditory: relating to the sense of hearing
4. diction: the clearness with which someone says words when speaking
5. indict: to say formally that someone has committed a crime.
6. contradict: to say that something is not true, or say that the opposite is true

Read & Replace

ROOTS are groups of letters that can be found at the beginning, middle, or end of a word. Each root has its own meaning. The root *aud* at the beginning of the word *audience* means *hear*. The root *dict* at the end of the word *predict* means *say*. READ the story. FILL IN the blanks with keywords.

audible	audience	audio	audition	auditorium
dictate	dictator	dictionary	predict	verdict

Neil's knees were shaking as he walked into the 1 _____.
He couldn't 2 _____ how the band would feel about him,
and he was nervous that his 3 _____ wouldn't go well.

Neil watched as the band's manager barked orders at everyone.
"This guy is a real 4 _____," he thought.

When it was his turn, Neil started to sing, but the 5 _____
knob on the microphone was turned too low. Someone fixed it
so that Neil's voice was 6 _____. Neil sang a few lines.
"Enough!" yelled the manager. "Have you got anything else to
show us?"

Neil waited for hours to hear the band's 7 _____. When
they said Neil had been chosen to be a member, he could hardly
believe it. But Neil knew he could never listen to anyone
8 _____ the way he should sing. He'd rather wait for his
chance to sing in front of a big 9 _____. He turned to the
manager and said, "You need to
learn about manners. You can start
by looking in the 10 _____
under the letter 'M.'" Then he
proudly walked away.

Root It Out

READ each definition. WRITE the missing root letters in the blanks.

HINT: Match the **bold** words in each definition to a root.

> *aud* = hear   *dict* = say

1. Someone who **says** what other people should do:
   __ __ __ __ator

2. A place where you can **hear** school announcements:
   __ __ __itorium

3. The jury foreman **says** the jury's decision or:
   ver__ __ __ __

4. If you can **hear** a whisper, it's
   __ __ __ible

5. A book that **tells** where words come from and what
   they mean:
   __ __ __ __ionary

6. The track of sound you can **hear** on a movie:
   __ __ __io

7. What a fortuneteller does when she **says** what will
   happen next year:
   pre__ __ __ __

8. The people who **hear** a band play:
   __ __ __ience

9. When you **say** your notes to a friend who copies
   them down, you
   __ __ __ __ate

10. When someone **hears** you play drums to tell if you
    are good enough join the band, it is an
    __ __ __ition

Combo Mambo

MATCH a word or ending in an orange box to a root in a yellow box to make a word. WRITE the word in the root box. Then LOOK UP the definition for each word and WRITE it in a sentence.

aud/audio = hear   *dict* = say or tell

ion	in	visual	contra	it	itory

AUD/AUDIO

_____

_____

_____

DICT

_____

_____

_____

_____

_____

_____

_____

_____

_____

_____

_____

_____

Criss Cross

FILL IN the grid by answering the clues with keywords.

ACROSS

3. The crowd at a concert

6. The place where you watch the school play

7. A sound that you can hear

8. A leader who makes all the rules

DOWN

1. To say that something will happen before it does

2. An opinion about something

4. A short performance to try out for something

5. Relating to sound

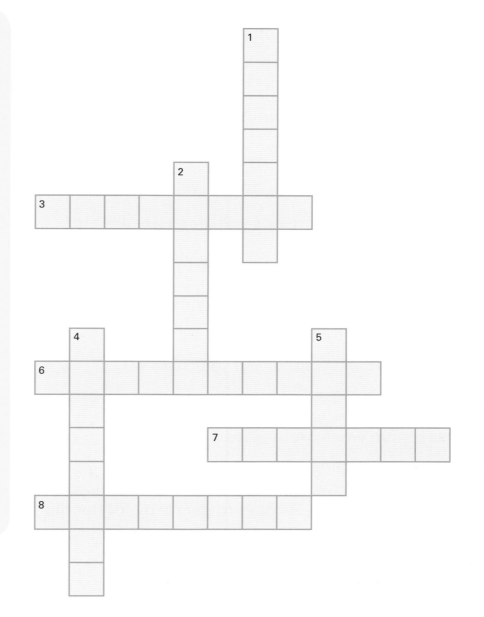

Blank Out!

FILL IN the blanks with keywords.

audible	audience	audio	audition	auditorium
dictate	dictator	dictionary	predict	verdict

1. Dolphins make sounds that are _____ underwater.

2. We can meet in the _____ to practice for the talent show.

3. I _____ that it will be sunny tomorrow.

4. It's hard to be friends with Peter. He likes to _____ everything we do.

5. The _____ was very quiet during the tennis match.

6. Lauren looked in the _____ to find the meaning of the word audiologist.

7. Lucas can't wait to hear the coach's _____ about who will make the team.

8. It's fun when Mom plays an _____ book for us in the car.

9. No one will want to be friends with you if you act like a _____.

10. Tina practiced for days to get ready for her big _____.

It's Puzzling!

MATCH a prefix, root, and suffix together to form a word. Then WRITE the words in the blanks.

HINT: You can use the same prefix, root, or suffix more than once.

Prefixes   **Roots**   **Suffixes**

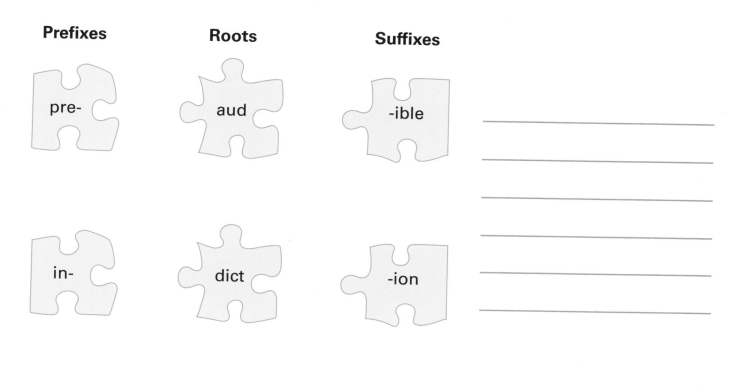

Blank Out!

FILL IN the blanks with keywords.

1. This word describes the bossiest person you know. _____

2. This word describes the voice on the other end of the telephone.

   _____

3. This book can help you learn to pronounce *glockenspiel*. _____

4. When you guess which team is going to win tomorrow's game,

   you _____.

5. The fans who are watching the game on television. _____

6. Your MP3 player is an _____ device.

7. This is what you need to do to try out for the chorus. _____

8. This is what the jury says when they decide whether someone is guilty or not.

   It is their _____.

9. My sister thinks she can _____ everything I should do.

10. This is the place everyone meets for an assembly. _____

Keywords

com•mand—kuh-MAND *verb* 1. to give orders 2. to have control over 3. to demand what you deserve

de•mand—dih-MAND *verb* 1. to ask for something firmly and forcefully 2. to need or require

de•scribe—dih-SKRIB *verb* to use words to tell about the details of someone or something

in•scrip•tion—ihn-SKRIHP-shun *noun* words or letters that are written, printed, or engraved as a lasting record

ma•neu•ver—muh-NOO-ver *noun* 1. a skillful move or action 2. a planned movement of military troops or ships 3. an action done to get an advantage

ma•nip•u•late—muh-NIHP-yuh-layt *verb* 1. to operate or use by hand 2. to manage or use with skill 3. to control or influence somebody, usually in order to deceive

man•u•al—MAN-yoo-uhl *adjective* 1. relating to or involving the hands 2. relating to work that requires physical effort 3. operated or powered by human effort

man•u•script—MAN-yuh-skrihpt *noun* 1. a book or document that is written by hand 2. a version of a book, article, or document submitted for publication

scrib•ble—SKRIHB-uhl *verb* to write something quickly and carelessly

sub•scribe—suhb-SKRIB *verb* 1. to pay for something that you will receive over a period of time, such as a magazine 2. to support or give approval to something as if by signing

✓ Check It!

Page 204
Read & Replace

1. subscribe
2. inscription
3. command
4. describe
5. manual
6. manipulate
7. manuscript
8. maneuver
9. scribble
10. demand

Page 205
Root It Out

1. manual
2. inscription
3. command
4. scribble
5. manipulate
6. describe
7. maneuver
8. subscribe
9. demand
10. manuscript

Page 206
Combo Mambo

1. manage: to handle or keep control of something
2. manicure: a treatment for the hands and nails
3. manufacture: to make something into a finished product
4. scripture: sacred writings
5. scriptwriter: someone who writes scripts for a movie or TV show
6. scriptural: relating to sacred writings

Read & Replace

The root *man* at the beginning of the word *manual* means *hand*. The root *scribe* at the end of the word *subscribe* means *write*. Read the story. FILL IN the blanks with keywords.

> command   demand   describe   inscription   maneuver
> manipulate   manual   manuscript   scribble   subscribe

Jeremy told his grandmother that he wanted to 1 _____ to a history magazine. He opened the mailbox and saw the magazine with a card. The 2 _____ on the card read, "To Jeremy, with love, Grandma."

On the cover, there was a photo of a general who looked like he was going to 3 _____ his men to fight. Inside, Jeremy saw an article that tried to 4 _____ what life was like at the time of the Revolutionary War. It told about all the hard 5 _____ work the soldiers had to do each day. Jeremy liked the step-by-step photos that showed how blacksmiths used hammers to 6 _____ iron. There was also a 7 _____ of a general's letter that had been dug up at the battleground, and a diagram of a 8 _____ the general had drawn out for his troops.

Jeremy started to 9 _____ some notes. He couldn't wait to learn more. He was just going to have to 10 _____ that his big sister log off the computer immediately!

Root It Out

LOOK AT each definition. WRITE the missing root letters in the blanks.

HINT: Some roots have alternate spellings.

> *man* = hand   *scribe* = write

1. Work that you need to use your **hands** to do is ___ ___ ___ual labor.

2. Words someone **writes** at the beginning of your book is an

   in ___ ___ ___ ___ ___tion.

3. If you **hand over** orders to someone, you com ___ ___ ___d them.

4. If you **write** quickly and sloppily, you ___ ___ ___ ___ ___ble.

5. You use your **hands** to do this to puzzle pieces: ___ ___ ___ipulate them.

6. When you **write** an e-mail to tell your friend all about your new pet iguana, you

   de ___ ___ ___ ___ ___ ___ it.

7. When you use your **hands** to do a cartwheel, you are doing a gymnastics

   ___ ___ ___euver.

8. When you sign up for **written** materials like a newspaper, you

   sub ___ ___ ___ ___ ___ ___ to it.

9. When you make a forceful or heavy-**handed** request, you

   de ___ ___ ___d something

10. Something that you **write** by **hand** is a ___ ___ ___u___ ___ ___ ___ ___ ___.

Combo Mambo

MATCH a word or ending in a red box to a root in an orange box to make a word. WRITE the word in the root box. Then LOOK UP the definition for each word and WRITE it in a sentence.

man = hand / *scribe* = write

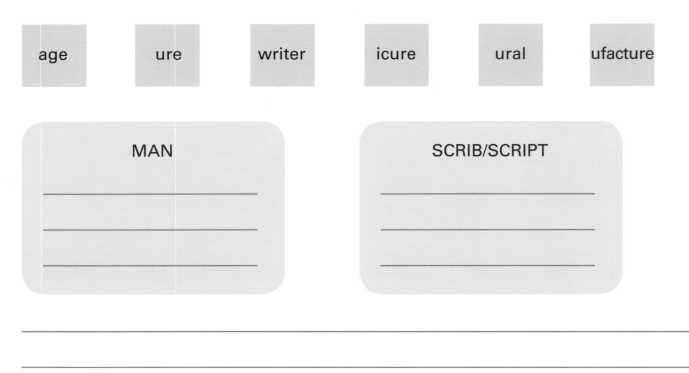

| age | ure | writer | icure | ural | ufacture |

MAN

_____

_____

_____

SCRIB/SCRIPT

_____

_____

_____

_____

_____

_____

_____

_____

_____

_____

Criss Cross

FILL IN the grid by answering the clues with keywords.

ACROSS

2. To ask for firmly

7. To use with skill

8. To write sloppily

9. To pay to have something delivered over a period of time

10. Words that are engraved on something

DOWN

1. Powered by human effort

3. To tell about the details of something

4. To have control over

5. A skillful move

6. A document submitted for publication

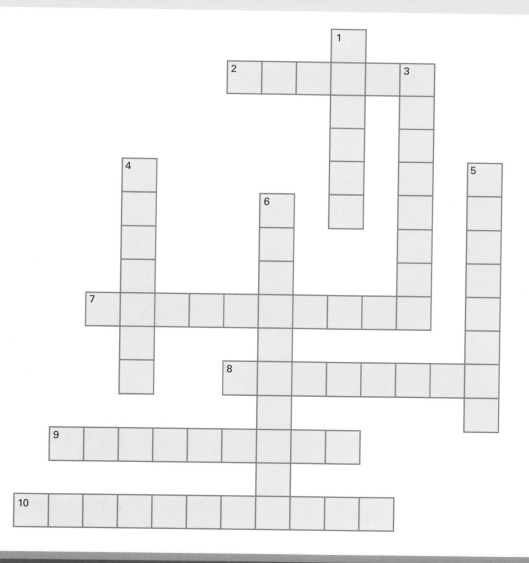

Blank Out!

FILL IN the blanks with keywords.

command	demand	describe	inscription	maneuver
manipulate	manual	manuscript	scribble	subscribe

1. Cleaning up your room is a _____ job.

2. A wheelie is a bicycle _____.

3. If you _____ your notes, you may not be able to read them later.

4. Jaden wrote a poem to _____ what it's like to sail.

5. It's not nice to _____ presents for your birthday.

6. Cassie's big brother tried to _____ her into doing his chores.

7. If you _____ to the extreme sports magazine, you'll get a copy every month.

8. When you write a story, make sure to keep a copy of the _____.

9. Zoe had an _____ from her dad on her locket.

10. Brian though he could _____ his little brother to obey him.

It's Puzzling!

MATCH a prefix, root, and suffix together to form a word. Then WRITE the words in the blanks.

HINT: You can use the same prefix, root, or suffix more than once. Some of the ending pieces actually contain more than one suffix.

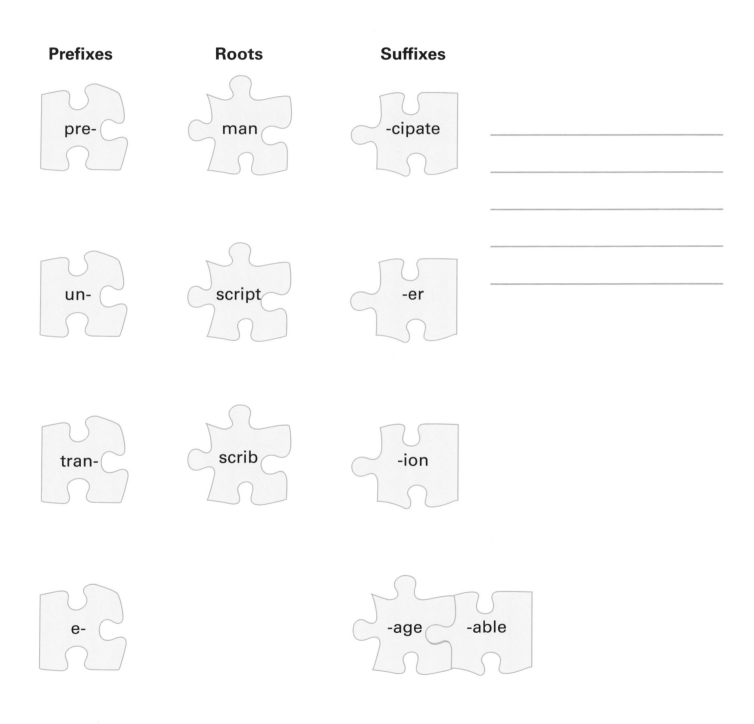

Prefixes

pre-

un-

tran-

e-

Roots

man

script

scrib

Suffixes

-cipate

-er

-ion

-age   -able

_____

_____

_____

_____

_____

Blank Out!

FILL IN the blanks with keywords.

1. This word tells how you get a newspaper delivered to your home. _____

2. This word is how you tell someone what your best friend looks like.

   _____

3. This word tells what you need to do to get a go-cart to work. _____

4. This word describes a version of a story you send in to be published by a

   magazine. _____

5. When you say, "I want a cookie right now!" you _____ it.

6. This word tells what you might have engraved on your jewelry box.

   _____

7. This word describes how you might doodle in the margin of your paper.

   _____

8. This word tells what you do when you say, "Everyone listen to me!"

   _____

9. When you dig with your hands, you are doing _____ work.

10. Pete used a fancy bike _____ down the tricky hill.

Keywords

gen•der—JEHN-der *noun* the male or female group that a person belongs to

gene—jeen *noun* a basic unit that holds characteristics that are passed from one generation to the next

gen•er•a•tion—jehn-uh-RAY-shuhn *noun* 1. the family members that are a step in line from a single ancestor 2. a group or people born and living at the same time 3. the average length of time it takes for people, animals, or plants to grow up and produce their own offspring

gen•er•ous—JEHN-er-uhs *adjective* 1. willing to freely give or share money, help, or time 2. having very high qualities, noble 3. large in size or quantity

in•nate—ih-NAYT *adjective* relating to qualities or abilities that you are born with

na•tion•al•i•ty—nash-uh-NAL-ih-tee *noun* 1. the state of belonging to a country or nation 2. a group of people who have a common beginning, tradition, or language

na•tive—NAY-tihv *adjective* 1. born in a specific place or country 2. born with; natural 3. grown, made, or having a beginning in a particular region

nat•u•ral—NACH-er-uhl *adjective* 1. present in or made by nature, rather than people 2. relating to nature 3. relating to something you are born with 4. not artificial

re•gen•er•ate—rih-JEHN-uh-rayt *verb* 1. to create or produce again 2. to give new life to 3. to replace a lost part with a new growth

su•per•nat•u•ral—soo-per-NACH-er-uhl *adjective* 1. relating to something that cannot be explained by natural laws 2. outside what is usual or normal

✓ Check It!

Page 212
Read & Replace

1. gene
2. native
3. regenerate
4. innate
5. gender
6. generation
7. generous
8. supernatural
9. nationality
10. natural

Page 213
Root It Out

1. gender
2. innate
3. supernatural
4. generation
5. native
6. natural
7. gene
8. nationality
9. generous
10. regenerate

Page 214
Combo Mambo

1. generate: to bring something into existence
2. genetics: the branch of science that deals with traits inherited through genes
3. genealogy: the study of the history of families
4. nation: a community of people who live in a defined area
5. naturalize: to give citizenship to somebody who is not a native
6. naturally: in a normal manner

Read & Replace

Here are some more roots to add to your collection. The root *gen* at the beginning of the word *gender* means *birth*. The root *nat* in the middle of the word *supernatural* means *born*.

READ the diary entry. FILL IN the blanks with keywords.

gender	gene	generation	generous	innate
nationality	native	natural	regenerate	supernatural

Dear Diary,

My lab experiment was a success! I was finally able to combine the 1 _____ of a pig with one from an iguana. The iguana, a 2 _____ of South America, is able to 3 _____ body parts. The pig is an animal that has 4 _____ intelligence. The new creature, which I call a piguana, makes a great pet. It is smaller than a pig, but it's very smart. If it gets hurt, it can regrow a new part. Soon I'll be able to offer them to pet shops in either 5 _____ —male or female. I am excited to be a part of a 6 _____ of scientists who are doing creative lab work. But I couldn't have done this without the 7 _____ help of my assistant, Igor. Some people have called the piguana a monster. They say we have used 8 _____ powers to do our work. Perhaps it is because of my Transylvanian 9 _____.
But these claims are untrue. It is completely 10 _____ to want to push science to its limits.

Dr. Frankenfeld

Root It Out

READ each definition. WRITE the missing root letters in the blanks.

HINT: Some roots have alternate spellings.

gen = birth   *nat* = born

gender	gene	generation	generous	innate
nationality	native	natural	regenerate	supernatural

1. Whether you're a girl or boy at **birth**, that's your ___ ___ ___ der.

2. An ability you were **born** with is in ___ ___ ___ ___.

3. Something that is **born** outside of natural laws is considered

   super ___ ___ ___ ural.

4. A group of people that share similar **birth** years are part of a ___ ___ ___ eration.

5. Someone who was **born** in this country is a ___ ___ ___ ive.

6. Something that is **born** in nature and not created in a lab is ___ ___ ___ ural.

7. Scientists are trying to figure out if a ___ ___ ___ e you have at **birth** can

   determine if you might get a disease.

8. A group of people who were **born** in a common place have the same

   ___ ___ ___ ionality.

9. If you have a noble spirit from **birth**, you are ___ ___ ___ erous.

10. To regrow or give **birth** to a lost part: re ___ ___ ___ erate

Combo Mambo

MATCH a word or ending in a blue box to a root in a green box to make a word. WRITE the word in the root box. Then LOOK UP the definition for each word and WRITE it in a sentence.

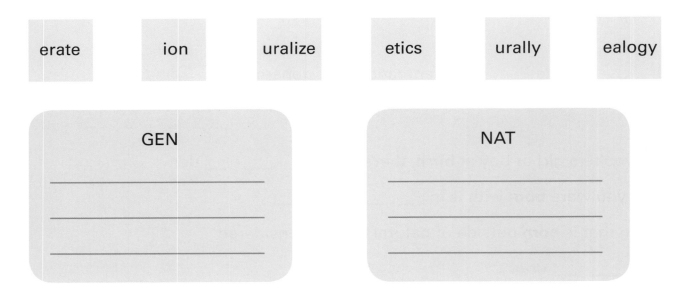

erate   ion   uralize   etics   urally   ealogy

GEN
_____
_____
_____

NAT
_____
_____
_____

_____
_____
_____
_____
_____
_____
_____
_____
_____

Criss Cross

FILL IN the grid by answering the clues with keywords.

ACROSS

2. The length of time between the birth of parents and the birth of their offspring
4. Outside of what is normal
5. Not artificial
6. Born in a particular place

DOWN

1. The part of DNA that holds information that has been passed down from each parent
3. To create again
5. The state of belonging to a nation

Blank Out!

FILL IN the blanks with keywords.

gender	gene	generation	generous	innate
nationality	native	natural	regenerate	supernatural

1. Fred prefers _____ juice to the kind made with artificial flavors.

2. Brenda believes she has _____ powers and can read other

   people's minds.

3. Does a _____ determine whether you are shy or not?

4. Nestor's dad was a piano player, so his musical ability must

   be _____.

5. It is very _____ to give your bed to your sister's friend during

   a sleepover party.

6. Chloe had a flag printed on her T-shirt to show her _____.

7. An iguana can _____ a new tail.

8. A new _____ of extreme athletes is ready to compete

   with the older crowd.

9. There are male and female athletes, so people of either

   _____ can be great athletes.

10. We asked Kevin to show us around New York City

    because he is a _____ New Yorker.

It's Puzzling!

MATCH a prefix, root, and suffix together to form a word. Then WRITE the words in the blanks.

HINT: If you get stuck, use a dictionary. Some of the ending pieces actually contain more than one suffix.

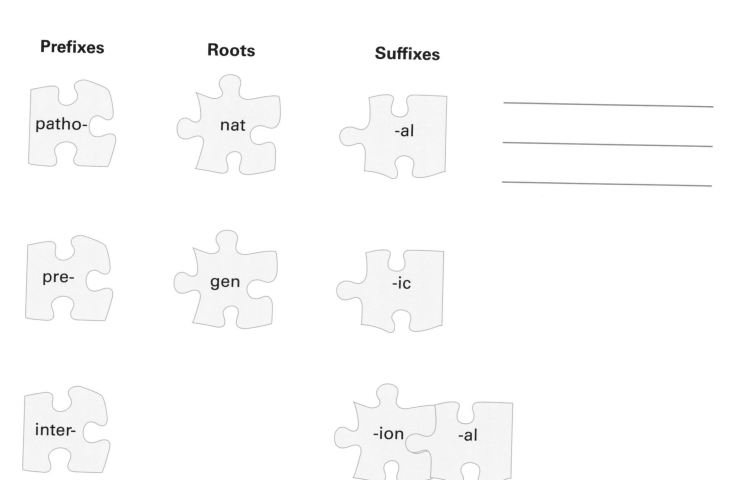

Prefixes

patho-

pre-

inter-

Roots

nat

gen

Suffixes

-al

-ic

-ion   -al

Blank Out!

FILL IN the blanks with keywords.

1. Orange juice that you squeezed from an orange is _____.

2. The difference between men and women is _____.

3. Some animals _____ a limb when they need to grow a new one.

4. All of the kids in your grade are a part of the same _____.

5. If you are a great tennis player, just like your mother, the ability is

   _____.

6. If you still live in the town where you were born, you're a _____.

7. Ghosts and goblins are _____.

8. Citizenship is another word for _____.

9. Your eye color is determined by a _____.

10. If you give all your old baseball cards to your sister, you are _____.

Keywords

de•fine—dih-FIN *verb* 1. to give a precise meaning of 2. to describe something clearly 3. to mark the limits of

def•i•nite—DEHF-uh-niht *adjective* 1. having fixed limits 2. clear in meaning 3. certain and unlikely to change plans

fi•nal•ize—FI-nuh-liz *verb* to put in final form

fi•nite—FI-nit *adjective* 1. with an end or limit 2. with a countable number of parts

il•lit•er•ate—ih-LIHT-er-iht *adjective* 1. having little or no education 2. being unable to read

in•fi•nite—IHN-fuh-niht *adjective* 1. without any limits or end 2. immeasurably great in size or number

lit•er•a•cy—LIHT-er-uh-see *noun* the ability to read and write

lit•er•al—LIHT-er-uhl *adjective* 1. true to fact 2. following the usual meaning of words 3. done word for word

lit•er•ar•y—LIHT-uh-rehr-ee *adjective* 1. relating to written works or writing as a profession 2. well read

lit•er•a•ture—LIHT-er-uh-choor *noun* written works such as books, poetry, and plays that are known for their excellence

✓ Check It!

Page 220
Read & Replace

1. literature
2. illiterate
3. infinite
4. definite
5. literal
6. literary
7. define
8. finalize
9. literacy
10. finite

Page 221
Root It Out

1. literature
2. define
3. literary
4. finite
5. literacy
6. finalize
7. illiterate
8. literal
9. infinite
10. definite

Page 222
Combo Mambo

1. finalist: someone who gets to the final rounds of a competition
2. finish: to come to an end
3. finally: after a long period of time
4. literalism: sticking strictly to the basic meaning of a word or story
5. literal: the exact meaning of a word
6. literalize: to make literal

Page 223
Criss Cross

ACROSS
2. illiterate
5. definite
7. finalize
8. literacy

DOWN
1. define
3. infinite
4. literal
6. literary

Read & Replace

The root *fin* in the middle of the word *definite* means *end*. The root *liter* at the beginning of the word *literature* means *letters*. Read the script. FILL IN the blanks with keywords.

define	definite	finalize	finite	infinite
illiterate	literal	literary	literature	literacy

Johnny: Hello?

Salesperson: Hi. I have a collection of fine 1_____ that I'd like to offer you today.

Johnny: No thank you. I'm 2_____, so I can't read.

Salesperson: But there are an 3_____ number of uses for this collection. You can use them as hot plates.

Johnny: I'm sorry, but my answer is a 4_____ no.

Salesperson: You're only thinking about the 5_____ meaning of my words. With this collection, you'll look like a real 6_____ genius.

Johnny: Do I have to 7_____ no for you?

Salesperson: Let's just 8_____ this deal now. You seem like you really need these books.

Johnny: Look, it's great that you care about 9_____. I was only joking, I can read well. But I have a 10_____ amount of patience. [click]

Root It Out

LOOK AT each definition. WRITE the missing root letters in the blanks.

1. Writers use **letters** to create these great books. __ __ __ __ __ ature

2. When you mark the **end** or boundary of a space, you de __ __ __ e it.

3. If you work by writing **letters**, words, and sentences, you have this kind of job.

   __ __ __ __ __ ary

4. Every year has an **end** so it is __ __ __ ite.

5. The skills you need to put **letters** together to read words.

   __ __ __ __ __ acy

6. When your conversation comes to an **end** and you agree on a decision.

   fin __ __ __ __ __ it.

7. If someone does not know the **letters** of the alphabet and cannot read, she is

   il __ __ __ __ __ ate.

8. If you read the **letters** of a word and only think about its exact meaning, you are

   being __ __ __ __ __ al.

9. You can't finish counting numbers without an **end** because they are

   in __ __ __ ite.

10. If you can clearly see the **ends** of something, it is de __ __ __ ite.

Combo Mambo

MATCH a word or ending in a blue box to a root in a red box to make a word. WRITE the word in the root box. Then LOOK UP the definition for each word and WRITE the word in a sentence.

fin = end   *liter* = letters

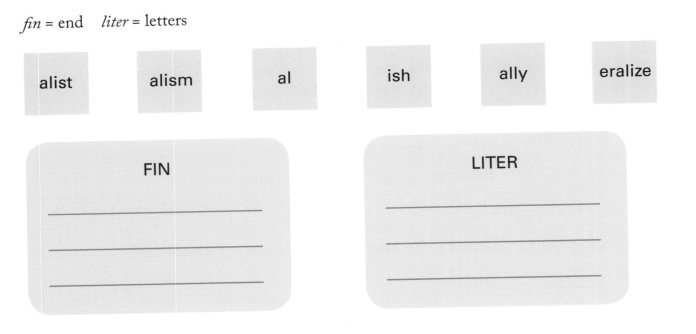

alist   alism   al   ish   ally   eralize

FIN

_____

_____

_____

LITER

_____

_____

_____

_____

_____

_____

_____

_____

_____

_____

_____

Criss Cross

FILL IN the grid by answering the clues with keywords.

ACROSS

2. Not able to read

5. Unlikely to change

7. To put in finished form

8. The ability to read and write

DOWN

1. To mark the limits of

3. Without limits

4. Exactly as said or written

6. Well-read

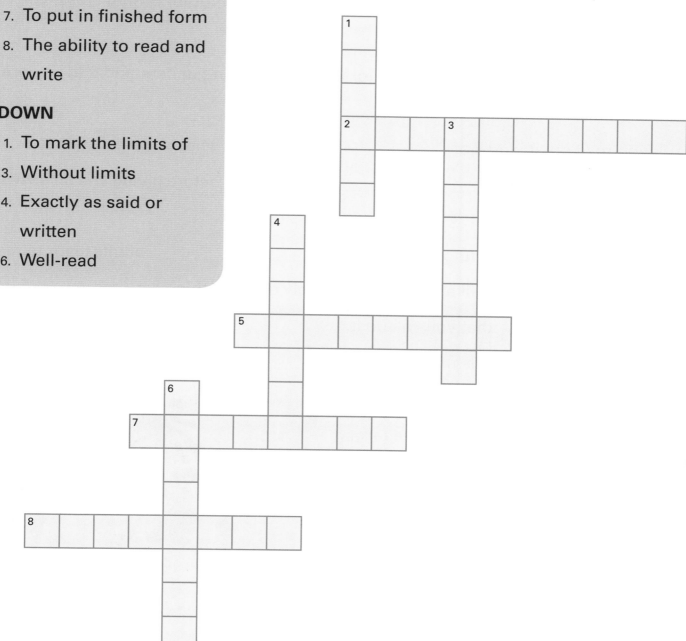

Blank Out!

FILL IN the blanks with keywords.

define	definite	finalize	finite	infinite
illiterate	literal	literary	literature	literacy

1. If you draw a line in the middle of the room that your brother cannot cross, you
   _____ a boundary.

2. If a friend takes what you say word for word and doesn't understand that you are
   joking, he is being _____.

3. If you read great works of _____, you'll be considered well read.

4. Victoria was waiting to _____ her plans before giving Joe an answer.

5. An author has a _____ profession.

6. Hans volunteered as a tutor to help teach _____ adults learn to read.

7. If you know that you will absolutely, positively do something, you are
   _____ that you will do it.

8. If you can see both ends of a line, it is _____.

9. If you talk about the number of kids
   you know who can read, you are talking
   about your friends' _____.

10. Walter has an _____
    amount of love for his grandpa.

It's Puzzling!

MATCH a prefix, root, and suffix together to form a word. Then WRITE the words in the blanks.

HINT: You can use the same prefix, root, or suffix more than once.

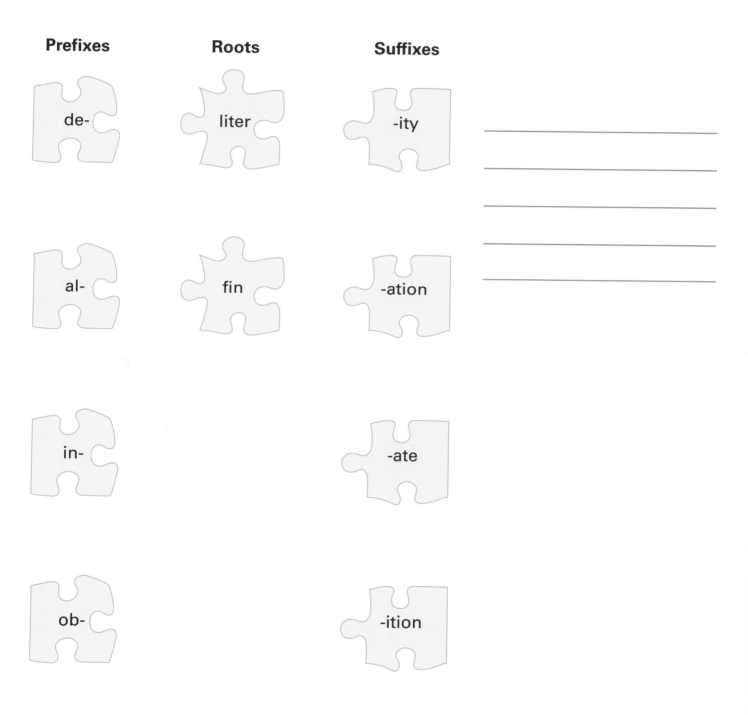

Prefixes   **Roots**   **Suffixes**

de-   liter   -ity

al-   fin   -ation

in-   -ate

ob-   -ition

Blank Out!

FILL IN the blanks with keywords.

define	definite	finalize	finite	infinite
illiterate	literal	literary	literature	literacy

1. This word tells how many grains of sand there are on the beach.

   _____

2. This word describes someone who does not know how to read.

   _____

3. If you have no doubts about going to the movie on Friday, your plans are

   _____.

4. This word is what you do when you decide with your friends exactly what movie

   you will see. _____

5. This word describes the number of days in a year. _____

6. This word describes the written works in a library. _____

7. This word describes the meaning of something exactly as it is written.

   _____

8. This word means the ability to read and write. _____

9. This word describes the type of person you are if you read a lot of books.

   _____

10. This word tells what you do when you say what a word means. _____

Pick the One!

You know your root words, right? So get going and check your skills! LOOK AT each group of words. CIRCLE the actual English word in each row.

1.	audible	audograph	inaudate
2.	dictalize	dictator	dictite
3.	unnational	nationor	nationality
4.	geneful	generation	genation
5.	nonsense	subsense	unsense
6.	maniture	manipulate	maniscribe
7.	illiterate	unliterate	reliterate
8.	infinite	prefinite	disfinite

Combo Mambo

WRITE all the words you can make by adding the suffixes to the roots.

HINT: Some roots are used more than once.

Root

fin

aud

liter

dict

Suffix

ite

ate

al

ible

ator

ition

✓ Check It!

Page 227

Pick the One!

1. audible
2. dictator
3. nationality
4. generation
5. nonsense
6. manipulate
7. illiterate
8. infinite

Combo Mambo

1. final, finite
2. audible, audition
3. literate, literal
4. dictate, dictator

Page 228

Match Up!

1. f—audible, audience, audio, audition
2. h—dictate, dictator, dictionary, predict, verdict
3. e—manuscript, scribble, subscribe, describe
4. a—maneuver, manipulate, manual
5. g—innate, nationality, native, natural
6. b—gender, gene, generation, generous
7. c—literal, illiterate, literary, literature, literacy
8. d—define, definite, finalize, finite, infinite

Page 229

Pathfinder

(de)scribe
(pre)dict
(in)nate
(de)fine
(il)literate
(de)mand
(sub)scribe

Match Up!

Can you MATCH each root to its meaning? When you're done, WRITE three words that contain each root.

1. aud   ___   a. hand

2. dict   ___   b. birth

3. script   ___   c. letters

4. man   ___   d. end

5. nat   ___   e. write

6. gen   ___   f. hear

7. litera   ___   g. born

8. fin   ___   h. say

1. _____   _____   _____

2. _____   _____   _____

3. _____   _____   _____

4. _____   _____   _____

5. _____   _____   _____

6. _____   _____   _____

7. _____   _____   _____

8. _____   _____   _____

Pathfinder

The game's the same, only the roots change. Begin at START. When you get to a box with two arrows, pick the root that you can add to the prefix. If you make all the right choices, you'll end up at FINISH.

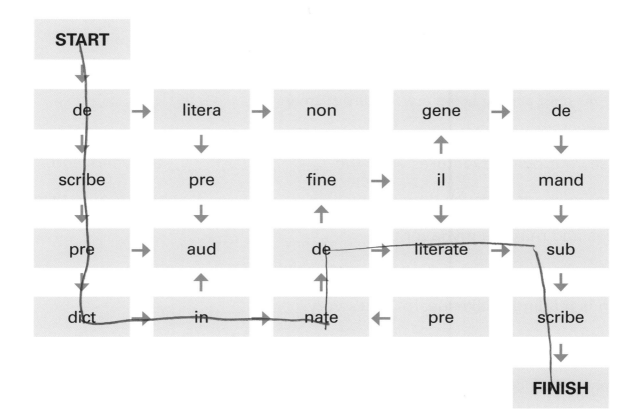

Sniglets!

You're not quite finished with sniglets yet! Here are some sniglets made with the roots you just reviewed.

litermature–the ability to read books that are challenging for your age
manibrate–the buzzing of a video game controller in your hand
audilogue–the conversation that happens when you talk to yourself
marscription–the doodles you write in the margins of your notebook
finifood–a bedtime snack, or the last thing you eat each day
genolit–the most popular books in a certain age group

WRITE a sniglet from the list to complete each sentence.

1. Choose your own adventures were the _____ ten years ago.

2. Samantha spent so much time on her _____she forgot to take notes.

3. Cookies and milk are my favorite _____.

4. It was embarrassing when Quentin overheard my _____.

5. Martin is reading Shakespeare. That's very _____.

6. Sometimes the _____ can be distracting when you're playing a game.

Now it's your turn. Here are some prefixes and roots you can use to create more sniglets.

Prefix	**Root**
ante- = before	hydro = water
contra- = against	matri = mother
hyper- = over, above	tempo = time
tele- = distance, from afar	vac = empty

_____

_____

_____

_____

ac•quire—uh-KWIR *verb* 1. to get as your own 2. to gain for yourself. Synonyms: get, gain, obtain. Antonyms: provide, give.

ap•proach—uh-PROHCH *verb* 1. to move closer to 2. to speak to someone in order to ask something. Synonyms: advance, move toward. Antonyms: retreat, pull back.

au•di•ble—AW-duh-buhl *adjective* able to be heard

au•di•ence—AW-dee-uhns *noun* a group that listens or watches

au•di•o—AW-dee-oh *adjective* 1. relating to sound that can be heard 2. relating to the recording or reproduction of sound

au•di•tion—aw-DIHSH-uhn *noun* 1. the sense of hearing 2. a test performance by a musician, singer, dancer, or actor

au•di•to•ri•um—awd-ih-TAWR-ee-uhm *noun* a building, or the area of a building, where the audience sits

bare—behr *adjective* 1. naked 2. exposed for all to see 3. empty

bear—behr *noun* a large mammal that has long shaggy hair and a short tail and eats both plants and meat *verb* 1. to hold up something heavy 2. to keep in one's mind

ben•e•fi•cial—behn-uh-FIHSH-uhl *adjective* 1. helpful 2. leading to good health and happiness. Synonyms: helpful, useful. Antonyms: harmful, destructive.

bright•ly—BRIT-lee *adverb* 1. in a way that gives off a lot of light 2. in a way that seems happy and cheerful

care•less—KAYR-lihs *adjective* 1. not paying careful attention to 2. done, made, or said without care

com•mand—kuh-MAND *verb* 1. to give orders 2. to have control over 3. to demand what you deserve

con•tent[1]—kuhn-TEHNT *adjective* satisfied with what you have

con•tent[2]—KAHN-tehnt *noun* 1. the amount of something inside something else 2. the subject or topic covered 3. the meaning or truth of a creative work

con•tract[1]—KAHN-trakt *noun* 1. a legal agreement between two or more people or groups

con•tract[2]—kuhn-TRAKT *verb* 1. to draw or squeeze together 2. to shorten or make smaller

damp•ness—DAMP-nuhs *noun* the quality of being slightly wet

de•fine—dih-FIN *verb* 1. to give a precise meaning of 2. to describe something clearly 3. to mark the limits of

def•i•nite—DEHF-uh-niht *adjective* 1. having fixed limits 2. clear in meaning 3. certain and unlikely to change plans

de•mand—dih-MAND *verb* 1. to ask for something firmly and forcefully 2. to need or require

de•scribe—dih-SKRIB *verb* to use words to tell about the details of someone or something

des•ert[1]—DEHZ-ert *noun* a land that is dry and has few plants

de•sert[2]—dih-ZERT *verb* 1. to go away from 2. to leave someone that you should stay with 3. to quit and leave without permission

dic•tate—DIHK-tayt *verb* 1. to speak or read for someone to write down 2. to give orders or rule over

dic•ta•tor—DIHK-tay-ter *noun* a leader who rules with total power over others

dic•tion•ar•y—DIHK-shuh-nehr-ee *noun* a reference book that lists words in alphabetical order and explains their meanings

dis•hon•est—dihs-AHN-ihst *adjective* lying, not honest

dis•please—dihs-PLEEZ *verb* to make someone feel dislike or annoyance

dis•sim•i•lar—dih-SIHM-uh-ler *adjective* different, unlike

end•less—EHND-lihs *adjective* 1. without end or limits 2. joined at the ends

e•nor•mous—ih-NAWR-muhs *adjective* unusually large in size or number. Synonyms: huge, massive, gigantic. Antonyms: tiny, small.

Vocabulary Words Index

en•ter•tain•ment—en-ter-TAYN-muhnt *noun* ways to give pleasure to or amuse people, such as singing, dancing, and acting

fair—fehr *noun* 1. a gathering of people who are buying and selling things 2. an event with rides, games, and competitions.
adjective 1. beautiful 2. clean or pure 3. not stormy or cloudy 4. likely to happen 5. not dark 6. neither good nor bad 7. in a way that is equal for everyone involved

fare—fehr *noun* 1. food 2. the money a person pays to travel by public transportation

fear•ful—FEER-fuhl *adjective* 1. filled with fear 2. nervous and easily frightened

feath•er•y—FEH*TH*-uh-ree *adjective* 1. like a feather 2. covered in feathers

fi•nal•ize—FI-nuh-liz *verb* to put in final form

fi•nal•ly—FIN-uhl-ee *adverb* 1. after a long period of time 2. happening at the end or last

fi•nite—FI-nit *adjective* 1. with an end or limit 2. with a countable number of parts

frac•ture—FRAK-cher *verb* to break. Synonyms: break, crack, rupture. Antonyms: fix, mend.

gen•der—JEHN-der *noun* the male or female group that a person belongs to

gene—jeen *noun* a basic unit that holds characteristics that are passed from one generation to the next

gen•er•a•tion—jehn-uh-RAY-shuhn *noun* 1. the family members that are a step in line from a single ancestor 2. a group or people born and   living at the same time 3. the average length of time it takes for people, animals, or plants to grow up and produce their own offspring

gen•er•ous—JEHN-er-uhs *adjective* 1. willing to freely give or share money, help, or time 2. having very high qualities, noble 3. large in size or quantity

gloom•y—GLOO-mee *adjective* 1. dark 2. sad. Synonyms: dark, unhappy, sad. Antonyms: bright, cheerful.

grad•u•al—GRAJ-ooh-uhl *adjective* moving or changing slowly in steps or degrees
Synonyms: slow, steady, regular. Antonyms: sudden, fast.

grate•ful—GRAYT-fuhl *adjective* having the desire to thank someone

heal—heel *verb* to make healthy

heel—heel *noun* 1. the back part of the foot below the ankle 2. the part of a shoe that covers the back of the foot 3. the lower, back, or end part 4. a person who is not nice. *verb* to make a person or animal obey

hu•mor•ous—HYOO-mer-uhs *adjective* funny. Synonyms: amusing, hilarious, funny. Antonyms: serious.

il•lit•er•ate—ih-LIHT-er-iht *adjective* 1. having little or no education 2. being unable to read

im•prove—ihm-PROOV *verb* to make or become better. Synonyms: get better, recover. Antonyms: worsen, deteriorate.

in•fi•nite—IHN-fuh-niht *adjective* 1. without any limits or end 2. immeasurably great in size or number

in•nate—ih-NAYT *adjective* relating to qualities or abilities that you are born with

in•quire—ihn-KWIR *verb* to ask about. Synonyms: ask, request. Antonyms: respond.

in•scrip•tion—ihn-SKRIHP-shun *noun* words or letters that are written, printed, or engraved as a lasting record

lit•er•a•cy—LIHT-er-uh-see *noun* the ability to read and write

lit•er•al—LIHT-er-uhl *adjective* 1. true to fact 2. following the usual meaning of words 3. done word for word

lit•er•ar•y—LIHT-uh-rehr-ee *adjective* 1. relating to written works or writing as a profession 2. well read

lit•er•a•ture—LIHT-er-uh-choor *noun* written works such as books, poetry, and plays that are known for their excellence

lo•cate—LOH-kayt *verb* 1. to find where something is 2. to put in a particular spot. Synonyms: place, find, discover. Antonyms: lose, misplace.

loud•ness—LOWD-nuhs *noun* 1. the degree of volume of sound

ma•neu•ver—muh-NOO-ver *noun* 1. a skillful move or action 2. a planned movement of military troops or ships 3. an action done to get an advantage

ma•nip•u•late—muh-NIHP-yuh-layt *verb* 1. to operate or use by hand 2. to manage or use with skill 3. to control or influence somebody, usually in order to deceive

man•u•al—MAN-yoo-uhl *adjective* 1. relating to or involving the hands 2. relating to work that requires physical effort 3. operated or powered by human effort

man•u•fac•ture—man-yuh-FAK-cher *verb* to make by hand or with machinery. Synonyms: make, produce, create. Antonyms: destroy, demolish.

man•u•script—MAN-yuh-skrihpt *noun* 1. a book or document that is written by hand 2. a version of a book, article, or document submitted for publication

mend—mehnd *verb* 1. to fix 2. to make better. Synonyms: repair, fix, recover. Antonyms: break, fracture.

mi•nus•cule—MIHN-uh-skyool *adjective* very small. Synonyms: tiny, minute, little. Antonyms: enormous, gigantic.

move•ment—MOOV-muhnt *noun* 1. the act of changing location or position 2. the way in which somebody or something moves

na•tion•al•i•ty—nash-uh-NAL-ih-tee *noun* 1. the state of belonging to a country or nation 2. a group of people who have a common beginning, tradition, or language

na•tive—NAY-tihv *adjective* 1. born in a specific place or country 2. born with; natural 3. grown, made, or having a beginning in a particular region

nat•u•ral—NACH-er-uhl *adjective* 1. present in or made by nature, rather than people 2. relating to nature 3. relating to something you are born with 4. not artificial

non•mov•ing—nahn-MOO-vihng *adjective* in a fixed position, not changing place or position

non•sense—NAHN-sehns *noun* silly or meaningless words or actions

non•tox•ic—nahn-TAHK-sihk *adjective* not poisonous, harmless

o•rig•i•nal—uh-RIHJ-uh-nuhl *adjective* 1. existing first 2. completely new and not copied. Synonyms: first, earliest, new. Antonyms: final, copy.

ob•ject[1]—AHB-jehkt *noun* 1. something that you can see and touch 2. something that is the target of your thoughts or feelings 3. the reason for doing something

ob•ject[2]—ahb-JEHKT *verb* to go against or oppose with firm words

pain•less—PAYN-lihs *adjective* 1. not causing pain 2. involving little difficulty

play•ful—PLAY-fuhl *adjective* 1. full of play, fond of playing 2. said or done in a fun way

pre•cau•tion—prih-KAW-shun *noun* something done beforehand to prevent harm

pre•dict—prih-DIHKT *verb* to tell what is going to happen in the future

pre•his•tor•ic—pree-hih-STAWR-ihk *adjective* relating to something that happened before written history

pre•school—PREE-skool *noun* the school a child attends before elementary school

pres•ent[1]—PREHZ-uhnt *noun* 1. something that is given to another 2. time that is happening now

pre•sent[2]—prih-ZEHNT *verb* 1. to introduce, to bring out before a group of people 2. to give

pre•view—PREE-vyoo *verb* to show or look at in advance

pro•vide—pruh-VID *verb* 1. to take care of 2. to supply what is needed. Synonyms: give, offer, supply. Antonyms: get, take.

pun•ish•ment—PUHN-ihsh-muhnt *noun* the act of punishing 2. a penalty for wrongdoing 3. rough treatment

re•ar•range—ree-uh-RAYNJ *verb* to put things in a new order or position

re•cent•ly—REES-uhnt-lee *adverb* relating to a time not long ago

Vocabulary Words Index

re•gen•er•ate—rih-JEHN-uh-rayt *verb* 1. to create or produce again 2. to give new life to 3. to replace a lost part with a new growth

re•play—ree-PLAY *verb* to play again

re•spond—rih-SPAHND *verb* 1. to answer 2. to react in response. Synonyms: reply, answer. Antonyms: ask, question.

re•view—rih-VYOO *verb* 1. to look at again 2. to report on the quality of something 3. to study or check again

scent—sehnt *noun* 1. an odor or smell 2. a sense of smell 3. hint 4. perfume

scrib•ble—SKRIHB-uhl *verb* to write something quickly and carelessly

sent—sehnt *verb* 1. caused to go 2. caused to happen

shad•ow•y—SHAD-oh-ee *adjective* 1. full of shadows 2. not clearly seen 3. not realistic

sly•ness—SLI-nuhs *noun* the quality of being sneaky or smart at hiding one's goals

sneak•y—SNEE-kee *adjective* doing things in a secret and sometimes unfair way

speed•i•ly—SPEED-uhl-ee *adverb* with quickness

sub•ma•rine—suhb-muh-REEN *noun* a vehicle that operates underwater

sub•scribe—suhb-SKRIB *verb* 1. to pay for something that you will receive over a period of time, such as a magazine 2. to support or give approval to something as if by signing

sub•top•ic—SUHB-tahp-ihk *noun* a topic that is a part of the main topic

sub•way—SUHB-way *noun* 1. a passage underneath the ground 2. an underground railway

suf•fi•cient—suh-FIHSH-uhnt *adjective* as much as needed. Synonyms: enough, plenty, ample. Antonyms: inadequate, poor.

su•per•nat•u•ral—soo-per-NACH-er-uhl *adjective* 1. relating to something that cannot be explained by natural laws 2. outside what is usual or normal

truth•ful—TROOTH-fuhl *adjective* honest, true, always telling the truth

un•com•fort•a•ble—uhn-CUHM-fert-uh-buhl *adjective* not feeling or giving comfort

un•like•ly—uhn-LIK-lee *adjective* not likely to happen

un•lim•it•ed—uhn-LIH-mih-tuhd *adjective* 1. without limits 2. having no boundaries or end. Synonyms: boundless, limitless. Antonyms: confined, bound.

un•u•su•al—uhn-YOO-zhoo-uhl *adjective* not common, rare

un•wise—uhn-WIZ *adjective* not wise, foolish

van•ish—VAN-ihsh *verb* 1. to disappear suddenly 2. to stop existing. Synonyms: disappear, go. Antonyms: appear, show.

ver•dict—VER-dihkt *noun* 1. the decision a jury reaches together 2. an opinion about something

weak—week *adjective* not strong

week—week *noun* the period of seven days that begins with Sunday and ends with Saturday

3rd-Grade
Reading Comprehension
Success

When you *predict*, that means you're guessing what the book is about before you read it. Smart readers predict before they read. Use the cover of a book to figure out what the story will be about.

Ask yourself what kind of story you are about to read. Is it a romance, science fiction, comedy, or mystery? These categories are called *genres*.

FILL IN the blank next to each cover with the genre you think it is.

science fiction   action   romance   horror

1. ~~romance~~

2. ~~action~~

3. ~~science fiction~~

4. ~~horror~~

✔ **Check It!**

Page 237

1. romance
2. action
3. science fiction
4. horror

Pages 238-239

Pick the One!

1. c
2. d
3. a
4. d
5. b
6. c

Pages 240-242

Doodle Pad

Suggested Titles:
1. Hot Dog Summer
2. Prairie Romance
3. Afraid to Fly
4. Kidnapped!
5. The Poodle Problem
6. Golf Dreams

Pages 243-244

Check, Please!

1. c
2. a
3. c
4. d
5. c
6. b

Pick the One!

CIRCLE the best title for each book cover.

1.
a. The Old Man and the Sea

b. The History of Baseball

c. A Boy and His Dog

d. School Stinks!

2.
a. High School Dance

b. The Popcorn Mystery

c. Rocketship Down!

d. Making the Team

3.
a. Call Me Mister Pimple!

b. Goldilocks and the Three Bears

c. Kyle the Cowboy Kid

d. Lost in the Mountains

4.

a. A Day in the Park

b. Summer Love

c. Going to Grandma's

d. Level Up!

5.

a. The Haunted House

b. Grounded for Life

c. Neighborhood Murder

d. Mrs. Frisby Moves Away

6.

a. Trapped with My Brother

b. I Hate Sisters!

c. Summer on Wheels

d. Ski Camp

Doodle Pad

CREATE a cover and title to match each plot.

Plot 1: Jeremy spends the summer with his grandma in a big house on Loony Lake. While he's there, he makes friends with Shania, the hot dog eating champion of Loony Lake. But at this year's hot dog eating contest, Jeremy is the winner! Will Shania still be his friend?

Title:

Plot 2: Starfire is a Native American girl. Johnny Kane is a young boy who's just joined the Pony Express to bring mail across the prairie. When Starfire saves Johnny from a robbery, they fall in love. Can two such different people find happiness?

Title:

Plot 3: In the mountain town of Belltoona, everyone's a pilot! The sky is filled with helicopters and mini-jets zipping through the air. Even the school bus has wings! But Chrissy Hepkins is afraid to fly. Will she face her fear or be the only kid in town riding a bike to school?

Title:

Plot 4: Twins Lucy and Andre are always fighting! Then one day, the twins are kidnapped by aliens from outer space. They have to get along and work together if they want to escape.

Title:

Predict & Confirm

Plot 5: Mayor MacBee's prized poodle has been dognapped. Everyone suspects crazy old Henry Hitchings. But Ricky "The Brain" Rodriguez isn't so sure. He's got to solve this mystery fast, before the wrong man goes to jail. The only problem: Ricky is in a wheelchair with two broken legs. Can he track down the missing poodle?

Title:

Plot 6: When Arnold Jackson makes the Junior Pro Golf League, it's a dream come true. He's going to be the next Tiger Woods! But then, his mom gets sick—real sick. If Arnold drops out of the league to help take care of her, what happens to his dream?

Title:

Check, Please!

CHECK the plot that's the best match to each cover.

1.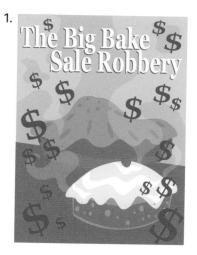

a. Thieves steal tons of gold bricks from Fort Knox.

b. A komodo dragon runs loose at a bake sale.

c. Gangsters steal the money from a church bake sale.

d. A little girl gets a new kitten.

2.

a. Jose's the best boarder on the hill until he's hurt in an accident.

b. Hillary and her brother fight over holiday candy.

c. Sanjay is accused of shoplifting, but it was really his friend Mike.

d. Maureen takes snowboarding lessons and becomes a champion.

3.

a. Candy Louis becomes a billionaire through babysitting.

b. A small town boy joins a famous rock band.

c. Missy Cooper lets her pop star fantasies get in the way of her real life.

d. A mother-daughter country music act travels all over the country.

Predict & Confirm

4.

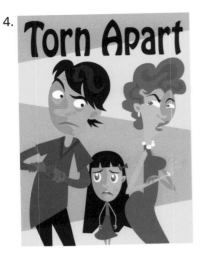

a. Betsy Johnson lost her cat and thinks her parents took it.

b. Isaac's parents want to know which one he likes better!

c. When Louisa's family plays Monopoly, the sparks fly!

d. Carlie's parents are getting divorced.

5.

a. Mickey's little brother is a real pest, so he decides to run away.

b. When Mickey was little, he was terrible, but he grew up okay.

c. The Santos family loses their dog on vacation, but he finds his way home!

d. Mickey is king of the dog world and must fight a mean enemy.

6.

a. A little boy is kidnapped by spies.

b. Isa may be too old for dolls, but she has to find Betty Lou!

c. Betty Lou is stuffed with dollar bills.

d. There's been a murder in Dollville!

✓ Check It!

Cut out the Check It! section on page 237, and see if you got the answers right.

Now you know that when you read FICTION, you try to *predict* what the story is about before you start. When you read NONFICTION, think about what you already know about the topic. Here's an example:

Topic: Getting a Pet

FILL IN the blanks with things you know about this topic.

1. **Kinds of Pets**

cats

dogs

ferrets

_____

2. **Pet Needs**

brushing

visits to the vet

exercise

_____

3. **Pet Stuff**

toys

food dish

bed

_____

✓ **Check It!**

Page 245

Suggestions:
1. hamsters
2. feeding
3. leash

Page 246

Suggestions:
1. glass bottles, plastic, containers, newspapers
2. electricity
3. plant a tree, replace your light bulbs with fluorescents
4. amusement parks, the beach, summer camp, a state park
5. shorts, tank tops, flip-flops, swimsuits
6. swimming, sun-tanning, volleyball, baseball
7. hot, humid, sunny, rainy

Page 248

Skimming

Suggestions:
1. basketball, soccer, golf, water polo
2. Michael Jordan, Mia Hamm, David Beckham, Derek Jeter
3. physical fitness, discipline, making friends
4. injuries, pressure, some kids don't like them

Page 249

Skimming

1. False
2. False
3. True
4. True
5. False
6. False
7. False
8. True

✓ Check It!

Page 251

Skimming

Suggestions:
1. color, sound, format (DVD)
2. Daniel Radcliffe, Cameron Diaz, Denzel Washington
3. *Toy Story, Harry Potter, The Incredibles*
4. movie theater, living room, airplane

Page 252

1. False
2. False
3. True
4. False
5. False
6. True
7. True
8. True

FILL IN the blanks with things you know about each topic.

Topic: Helping the Planet

1. **You Can Recycle**

metal cans

2. **Don't Waste**

gasoline

water

3. **Take Action**

pick up litter

turn out the lights

Topic: Summer

4. **Summer Vacation Places**

5. **Summer Clothes**

6. **Summer Activities**

7. **Summer Weather**

Skimming

When you SKIM an article, that means you don't read every word. Sometimes you might only read the *headings* (words in big, bold letters) and the picture captions. This is a good way to predict what you'll learn from the article! SKIM this article.

HINT: Notice anything funny about this page? We've already blurred the words you can skip.

Kids and Sports

The Most Popular Sports for Kids

Riusting ero euis augiuer sed min ullao sfiusting ero euis augiuer sed min ullao secte vert laorger cilit, consegu ancionum ex eugiearger cilit, consegu ancionum ex euguerc illamet dio consecten doloreet num deliquat aufio consecten doloreet num deliquat aut lummod te digna feum ex eu facium in et augiame digna feum ex eu facium in et augiam.

Kids Love Sports Heroes!

Riusting ero euis augiuer sed min ullao sfiusting ero euis augiuer sed min ullao secte vert laorger cilit, consegu ancionum ex eugiearger cilit, consegu ancionum ex euguerc illamet dio consecten doloreet num deliquat aufio consecten doloreet num deliquat aut lummod te digna feum ex eu facium in et augiame digna feum ex eu facium in et augiam.

Sports Are Good for Girls *and* Boys

Riusting ero euis augiuer sed min ullao sfiusting ero euis augiuer sed min ullao secte vert laorger cilit, consegu ancionum ex eugiearger cilit, consegu ancionum ex euguerc illamet dio consecten doloreet num deliquat aut lummod te digna feum ex eu facium in et augiam.

The Bad Side of Sports: Injury and Competition

Riusting ero euis augiuer sed min ullao secte vert laorger cilit, consegu ancionum ex euguerc illamet dio consecten doloreet num deliquat aut lummod Riusting ero euis augiuer sed min ullao secte vert laorger cilit, consegu ancionum ex euguerc illamet dio consecten doloreet num deliquat aut lummod te digna feum ex eu facium in et augiam.

Sometimes sports can lead to injuries.

FILL IN the blanks with things you think you would read about in the article you skimmed.

Topic: Sports

1. **Popular Sports**

baseball _____

_____

_____

_____

2. **Famous Names in Sports**

Tiger Woods _____

_____

_____

_____

3. **Good Things about Sports**

Sporty kids make good leaders. ____

_____

_____

_____

4. **Bad Things about Sports**

Sporty kids might skip homework. ___

_____

_____

READ each statement about the article you skimmed. CIRCLE *True* or *False* for each statement based on what you learned from skimming.

1. It's never good for kids to play sports.   True   False

2. There are only three sports that kids can play.   True   False

3. Kids may be hurt while playing sports.   True   False

4. Sports are popular with kids.   True   False

5. Girls aren't very good at sports.   True   False

6. Kids don't care about sports heroes.   True   False

7. There's nothing bad about sports for kids.   True   False

8. Competition can sometimes go too far.   True   False

Skimming

SKIM this article.

100 Years of Movies

From Silent Pictures to 3-D:
How the Movies Have Changed

Riusting ero euis auguer sed min ullaor secte vent laorper ollit, consequ amconum ex auguerc illamet laorper ollit, consequ amconum ex auguerc illamet dio consectem doloreet num deliquat aut lummod te digna feum ex eu facum in et augiam.

The Sky Is Filled with Stars:
Movie Stars

Riusting ero euis auguer sed min ullaor secte vent laorper ollit, consequ amconum ex auguerc illamet dio consectem doloreet num deliquat aut lummod dio consectem doloreet num deliquat aut lummod te digna feum ex eu facum in et augiam.

In the early days, movies didn't have color.

A Century of Famous Films

Riusting ero euis auguer sed min ullaor Riusting ero euis auguer sed min ullaor sed min ullaor sed laorper ollit, consequ amconum ex auglaorper ollit, consequ amconum ex augnconum ex auguerci dio consectem doloreet num deliquat audio consectem doloreet num deliquat anum deliquat aut lu te digna feum ex eu facum in et augiarte digna feum ex eu facum in et augiacum in et augiam.

Movies on the Move—
You Can Watch Them Anywhere!

Riusting ero euis auguer sed Riusting ero euis auRiusting ero euis auguer sed min ullaor secte vent laorper ollit, consequ amconularger ollit, conseqlaorger ollit, consequ amconum ex auguerc illamet dio consectem doloreet num dio consectem doldo consectem doloreet num deliquat aut lummod te digna feum ex eu facum in te digna feum ex eu eu digna feum ex eu facum in et augiam.

FILL IN the blanks with things you think you would read about in the article you skimmed.

Topic: Movies

1. Changes in Movies Over 100 Years

computerized special effects

_____

_____

_____

2. Famous Movie Stars

George Clooney

_____

_____

_____

3. Famous Movies

Star Wars

_____

_____

_____

4. Places You Can Watch Movies

minivan

_____

_____

_____

READ each statement about the article you skimmed. CIRCLE *True* or *False* for each statement, based on what you learned from skimming.

1. The movie business is failing.   True   False

2. Movies haven't changed much in 100 years.   True   False

3. There are lots of famous movie actors.   True   False

4. The first movies were in 3-D.   True   False

5. You can only watch movies in theaters.   True   False

6. Some movies have stayed famous for many years.   True   False

7. You can watch movies on an airplane.   True   False

8. Old movies didn't have color.   True   False

Check It!

Cut out the Check It! section on page 245, and see if you got the answers right.

You already know how to predict what a story is going to be about. And you know to confirm your guess after you're done reading. What's left? REVISE. That's right! You revise your prediction while you read. Here's how it works:

1. What do you think this story is about?

_____

_____

_____

_____

READ this paragraph from the story.

> Ernie held onto the branch with all his strength. If his fingers slipped, he would slide down the cliff and fall a hundred feet! Suddenly he heard a familiar sniffing sound, followed by a whine. Carefully Ernie looked up to see Daisy Dawg, wagging her tail at the edge of the cliff.
>
> "Daisy!" cried Ernie. "Am I glad to see you!"

2. Now what do you think this story is about?

_____

_____

_____

If you changed your mind, then you REVISED your prediction. A good story will always keep you guessing.

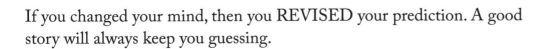

✓ Check It!

Page 253

1. The book could be about a boy who rescues a dog.
2. The story is about a dog that rescues a boy.

Page 254

1. The book might be about two kids who are being chased by a monster.
2. The book is about two kids whose identities and lives are erased, and they have to figure out why.

Pages 255-256
Stop & Go Story

Did you choose Yes or No?

Pages 257-258
Stop & Go Story

1. You might think Jake will use the money to buy a water gun.
2. You probably think Jake will use the money to buy a water gun.
3. You might think Jake will bring the money to the police.
4. You probably think Jake is going to use the reward to buy a water gun.

✓ Check It!

Page 259-260

Stop & Go Story

1. Coach Krantz might be mad because something bad happened to him.
2. Coach Krantz might be mad because his team lost the game.
3. Coach Krantz might be mad because the waitress spilled his coffee.
4. Coach Krantz is mad because he broke his toe

LOOK at the cover. FILL IN the blanks with your prediction about the story.

1. What do you think this story is about?

_____

_____

_____

_____

READ this paragraph from the story.

> It was like they didn't exist and never had. Their teacher at school had never heard of a Jake or Letty Sitwell. For some reason, their parents didn't recognize them. Suddenly Jake smiled. They could do anything they wanted, right? Right!
>
> But Letty was way ahead of him. "There's the bus to the mall," she said. "I need a smoothie if I'm gonna figure out this mystery."

2. Now what do you think this story is about?

_____

_____

_____

Stop & Go Story

READ each paragraph. Then CIRCLE the answer to each question.

GO

In their secret hideout under Grizzly Mountain, the SuperSpy Team watched a message from their leader, X. "I've got bad news for you, SuperSpies," X said. "It looks like Doc Rotten has made a machine to change the weather. He's going to freeze Hawaii and melt the North Pole. We've got to stop him!"

The entire team jumped to their feet. "Let's go!"

STOP

Can the SuperSpies stop Doc Rotten?

Yes   No

GO

SuperSpy M and her kid brother Q zipped through the sky in their SpyShuttle. "I see him!" yelled Q, pointing. "Wow, that weather machine is *big*." They shot at Doc Rotten with their StingRays, but Doc Rotten sent a giant swarm of moths to knock their SpyShuttle out of the sky.

"You are now my prisoners!" shouted Doc Rotten.

STOP

Can the SuperSpies stop Doc Rotten?

Yes   No

GO

"I'll deal with you later," snapped Doc Rotten, leaving M and Q tied up. Then he started powering up his weather machine. It glowed with a red light. "Time to start some global warming!" the evil mastermind cackled.

"We've got to stop him!" cried M, tugging at the ropes. As they struggled, they heard a strange sound.

"Is that the weather machine?" asked Q.

STOP

Can the SuperSpies stop Doc Rotten?   Yes   No

GO

"It sounds like—like barking!"cried M.

It *was* barking! In fact, it was SuperSpy K9, running across Doc Rotten's evil lair. She used the laser beam on her collar to cut the ropes around M and Q, then she jumped at Doc Rotten, growling and showing her big teeth. M and Q turned off the weather machine just in time. When Doc Rotten was behind bars, the team called SuperSpy X. "We did it!" they shouted.

STOP

Did the SuperSpies stop Doc Rotten?   Yes   No

Stop & Go Story

READ each paragraph. Then FILL IN the blanks to answer each question.

GO

It's Jake's birthday, but he's miserable. His parents did *not* give him a 3XL Turbo-Shooter water gun like he asked for. Walking down the sidewalk, Jake kicks a lump of dirt. Wait! That's not a lump of dirt. It's a wallet! Jake picks it up and looks inside. It's filled with twenty-dollar bills!

STOP

1. What do you think Jake will do with the wallet?

_____

_____

GO

Jake counts the money quickly. There's enough to buy *ten* Turbo-Shooters! And the toy store is only a few blocks away.

STOP

2. What do you think Jake will do with the wallet?

_____

_____

GO

Just then Jake's pal Steffie zooms up on her scooter. "Hey Jake!" she says. "Whatcha got there?" When she sees the wallet, her eyes get big. "Whoa!" she says. "You better bring that wallet to the police. I bet someone's looking for it. That's a lot of money to lose."

STOP

3. What do you think Jake will do with the wallet?

_____

_____

GO

Steffie and Jake take the wallet to the police station. Standing at the counter is a big man with a very red face. He looks upset. When Jake puts the wallet on the counter, the big man pounces on it.

"My wallet!" he cries. "I'm so glad you found it!" He opens it up and counts the bills. "It's all there! Thank goodness." The big man pulls out sixty dollars and hands it to Jake. "Thank you for being honest, my boy."

Jake knows just what to do next.

STOP

4. What do you think Jake will do with the reward?

_____

_____

Stop & Go Story

READ each paragraph. Then FILL IN the blanks to answer each question.

GO Coach Krantz was the nicest guy in town. But not today. Today the coach was *mad*. He yelled at the kids on the baseball team at morning practice. Then he snapped at the waitress in Joe's Diner at lunch. That afternoon he made a mean face when his neighbor waved at him and then slammed his front door.

STOP 1. Why do you think Coach Krantz is mad?

_____

_____

GO The kids on Coach Krantz's baseball team were worried. "I bet Coach is mad at us because we lost the big game," said Jordan. The other kids nodded sadly.

STOP 2. Why do you think Coach Krantz is mad?

_____

_____

GO Meanwhile, at the diner, Joe the cook found the waitress crying into her apron. "What's wrong?" he asked.

"Coach Krantz is mad at me," sniffled the waitress. "He's mad because I spilled his coffee at lunch today."

STOP 3. Why do you think Coach Krantz is mad?

_____

_____

GO After Coach Krantz made a mean face and slammed the door, his neighbor, Mrs. Ling, was surprised to see a whole bunch of baseball players and a waitress walk up to his house. "What's going on?" she asked.

"We're here to say we're sorry," said one of the baseball players. "We all made Coach mad today."

Mrs. Ling rang the bell. When Coach opened the door, they saw that his foot was wrapped in a big bandage. "Coach, what's wrong with your foot?" asked Mrs. Ling.

"I broke my big toe when I tripped over my own shoes," said the Coach. "I'm so mad—it's been killing me all day!"

STOP 4. Why do you think Coach Krantz is mad?

_____

_____

 **Check It!**

Cut out the Check It! section on page 253, and see if you got the answers right.

The best way to remember all the great information you're reading is to stop every now and then. That will give you the chance to think about what you just read and make a list in your head, or notebook, of what you learned. Give it a try.

Stop & Go Story

Growing Up Fast

How old does a doctor or a lawyer have to be? Not as old as you think. When Kathleen Holtz passed the California bar test to become a lawyer, she was only 18. That's right! She started college at 11, and entered law school at 15. And Balamurali Ambati became the world's youngest doctor at age 18.

STOP

1. What did you just learn?

_____

_____

GO

Other young professionals include film director Kishan Shrikanth (who made his first movie at age 10), cartoonist Alexa Kitchen (published at 7), and actress Anna Paquin (who won an Oscar when she was 11). Of course, when it comes to stuff like video games, kids rule! Victor De Leon III became a professional video gamer at age 9!

2. What did you just learn?

_____

_____

✓ Check It!

Page 261

Stop & Go Story

1. Someone became a lawyer at 18, started college at 11, and law school at 15. And the world's youngest doctor was 18.
2. There was a 10-year-old who directed a movie, a 7-year-old published cartoonist, an 11-year-old Oscar winner, and a 9-year-old professional video gamer.

Pages 262-263

Stop & Go Story

1. A roller coaster ride lasts about 2.5 minutes, the first big hill is called the "lift hill," and chains pull the cars up that hill.
2. Gravity and speed from the first hill can drive the roller coaster car for the rest of the ride.
3. Roller coaster cars can go as fast as 85 miles per hour on a steel structure. Wooden roller coasters only go as fast as 65 mph.
4. The brakes of most roller coasters aren't on the cars, they're on the tracks. The brakes are strong clamps that grab the car's wheels to slow them down.

Pages 264-265

Stop & Go Story

1. Some people get help from animals.
2. Seeing-eye dogs have been helping blind people for many years. Dogs can also tell by smell when a person needs medicine.
3. There are guide horses that help blind people who may be allergic to dogs. Horses also live longer than dogs.
4. There are helper monkeys that can open refrigerators and bring things to people who have to use a wheelchair.

Stop & Go Story

READ each paragraph. Then FILL IN the blanks to answer the question.

GO

A Wild Ride

A roller coaster ride may only last about 2.5 minutes, but there's a lot going on. At the start of the ride, your car needs to get up that first big hill, called the *lift hill*. Most of the time, there are chains pulling the cars up the lift hill (you can hear them clacking).

STOP

1. What did you learn about roller coaster rides?

_____

_____

GO

At the top of the lift hill, your coaster car lets go of the chains and gravity takes over. You slam through hills and turns and even loop-de-loops without any motors or electricity. Your car can run the whole ride using the speed it got from that first lift hill.

STOP

2. What did you learn about roller coaster rides?

_____

_____

GO

Roller coaster cars can go as fast as 85 miles per hour (over 135 kilometers per hour) if the entire ride is made of steel. But some roller coasters are made of wood. Wooden roller coasters can only go as fast as 65 mph (over 100 kilometers per hour). But they can *all* swish your stomach around!

STOP

3. What did you learn about roller coaster rides?

_____

_____

GO

Now it's time to hit the brakes. The brakes aren't usually on the cars, they're on the tracks. When the car comes to the end of the ride, strong clamps grab onto the wheels to slow them down. After braking, the car pulls into the station and the ride is over. Want to go again?

STOP

4. What did you learn about roller coaster rides?

_____

_____

Stop & Go Story

READ each paragraph. Then FILL IN the blanks to answer the question.

Helper Animals

Some people need help because they're blind or in a wheelchair or sick. But who wants to depend on another human all the time? That's why we have helper animals. With a helper animal, you take care of the animal, and the animal takes care of you. That's only fair, right?

1. What did you learn about helper animals?

_____

_____

Dogs have been helping blind people for many years. Seeing-eye dogs are specially trained to know how to cross busy streets and get through crowded sidewalks. Lately, scientists have learned that a dog's sense of smell is almost as good as a blood test. A dog can smell when some people are sick and can alert their human that it's time to take medicine. Pretty cool, huh?

2. What did you learn about helper animals?

_____

_____

GO

But dogs aren't the only helper animals. Some people are afraid of dogs or allergic to them. So there are also guide horses. That's right! Small breeds of horses, no taller than a grownup's hip, can also be trained to help a blind person get where they're going. Guide horses are better than dogs for people who don't want to keep their guide animal in the house. (Horses can live in a stable.) Plus, horses live a lot longer than dogs (40 years!), so you can train one to be with you for a long time.

3. What did you learn about helper animals?

_____

_____

GO

Neither dogs nor horses can open the refrigerator and bring a drink to a person in a wheelchair. So that's why there are also helper monkeys! Monkeys are really smart, and they have hands that can press buttons and carry things for people who can't. Monkeys, horses, and dogs help people every day. If you try, you can probably think of even more wonderful helper animals!

STOP

4. What did you learn about helper animals?

_____

_____

Stop & Go Story

READ each paragraph. Then FILL IN the blanks to answer the question.

Arthur Ashe

When Arthur Ashe was five, his father got a really cool job. He was caretaker of a big park in Richmond, Virginia. The family moved to a house right in the park. So they had a playground, a pool, and a bunch of tennis courts in their own backyard. Arthur learned to play tennis when he was very young, during a time when African Americans like himself were not even allowed to play tennis in certain places.

1. What did you learn about Arthur Ashe?

_____

_____

When Arthur was almost seven years old, a very sad thing happened. His mom died. He started to play tennis all the time, maybe because he missed her so much. But he also graduated at the top of his high school class and was the first member of the Ashe family to graduate from college.

2. What kind of *kid* was Arthur Ashe?

_____

_____

GO

All Arthur's tennis practice paid off. He became the first African-American man to be on the U.S. Davis Cup tennis team. He won the very first U.S. Open tennis tournament. And in 1975, Arthur Ashe was ranked the number one male tennis player in the whole world!

STOP

3. What did you learn about Arthur Ashe?

_____

_____

GO

But being a famous tennis player wasn't enough. While Arthur Ashe was growing up in Virginia, he saw black people treated differently than white people. That started to change as he got older. But in South Africa, it was still legal to treat black people badly. So Arthur became an activist—he spoke out against the government of South Africa. He went to South Africa as the first black professional tennis player, and the black South Africans called him "Sipho," which means "a gift from God."

STOP

4. What kind of *man* was Arthur Ashe?

_____

_____

Let's continue the story.

GO Then something terrible happened. Arthur had a heart attack! He had to stop playing tennis in 1980. A few years later, he needed an operation. At this time, people didn't know much about HIV or AIDS. Arthur got HIV from the blood they gave him during the operation. He talked to the press about his illness so that everyone would learn about HIV and AIDS, and he raised money to help find a cure.

STOP 5. What did you learn about Arthur Ashe?

_____

_____

GO Arthur Ashe died in February 1993. He was fifty years old. Almost 6,000 people attended his funeral in Richmond, Virginia, where they placed a statue of him on the town's famous Monument Avenue. Today, the main tennis court of the U.S. Open is called Arthur Ashe Stadium, after the first man (white or black) who won that tournament.

STOP 6. Why do you think so many people went to Arthur Ashe's funeral?

_____

_____

✓ Check It!

Cut out the Check It! to see if you got the answers right.

Reading is all about words, right? Wrong! While you read, you need to VISUALIZE. That means you make a picture in your head of what you're reading, like watching a movie!

READ each sentence, and CHECK the picture that matches it best.

1. Jack and Jill ran up the hill to fetch a pail of water.

a.  b. 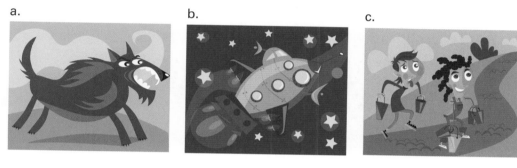 c.

2. Jack fell down the hill and a dinosaur ate him.

a.  b. c.

3. Jill grabbed her magic wand and turned the dinosaur into a butterfly.

a.  b.  c.

See how it works? Every good story makes a picture in your head.

4. Gerald lay in bed, watching the monster climb through his window.

a.   b.   c.

5. Marvin's father has a long black beard.

a.   b.   c.

6. Cindi woke up with a big, red pimple on her nose.

a.   b.   c.

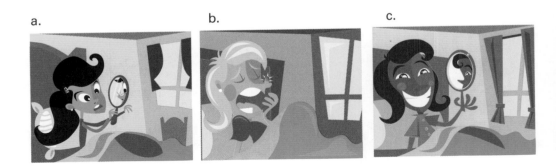

7. Baby kangaroos sleep in a pouch on their mother's belly.

a.   b.   c.

8. Our house was brand new, with big windows and a blue front door.

a.   b.   c.

9. Jimbo the Space Alien had bushy eyebrows, giant teeth, and a big smile.

a.   b.   c.

Doodle Pad

READ the paragraph and DRAW the picture it makes in your head.

Have you ever really looked at a fly? The common housefly can be up to half an inch long. Its wingspan is even longer! It has transparent wings, six jointed legs, and two giant red eyes on either side of its head. Behind the fly's head is its *thorax*, which is gray with four black stripes and shaped like a teardrop. Then comes its *abdomen*, which is a longer (kind of hairy) oval that ends in a stumpy little tail. Two tiny antennae stick out from between its eyes (where a human nose would be).

DRAW the common housefly here:

Doodle Pad

READ the paragraph and DRAW the picture it makes in your head.

On the first day of camp, we met our counselor, Trixie. She had lots of freckles, and red hair that she always wore in two short braids. Her smile was big and friendly, but her braces were usually full of whatever she ate for lunch. For some reason, Trixie liked to wear wild clothes that were way too big for her. And get this: She was always doing yo-yo tricks. Seriously! She could do anything with her crazy yo-yo. But everyone in my cabin liked her right away. We just knew she was cool, even if she looked a little weird!

DRAW Trixie here:

Doodle Pad

READ the paragraph and DRAW the picture it makes in your head.

Zeke opened his eyes. He was alive! The bright sun made his head ache. He turned over and felt sand beneath his hands. He was on a beach! All around him were pieces of the shipwreck: broken boxes, planks of wood, some furniture. The ocean stretched out forever. Zeke was thirsty. A few feet away, he saw some people sitting under a row of palm trees. Maybe those people had some water. He started to crawl across the sand toward the trees.

DRAW Zeke's story here:

Doodle Pad

READ the paragraph and DRAW the picture it makes in your head.

Every year since 1967, the Canadian city of Nanaimo has had a 36-mile bathtub race! The people who race (called *tubbers*) have to make their boats out of bathtubs. Serious tubbers build specially made tubs that fit inside real racing boats. Other tubbers get silly, dressing like mermaids or using rope to tie an ordinary bathtub onto a floating platform. No matter who wins the race, everyone has fun when the water is filled with bathtubs!

DRAW the Nanaimo bathtub race here:

Picture This!

Doodle Pad

READ the paragraph and DRAW the picture it makes in your head.

Standing on the tower, high above the front gate, Jared watched a band of men attack his father's castle. They were shooting arrows from their long bows at the men guarding the gate. The arrows bounced off the guard's shields. Meanwhile, some of his father's soldiers were heating up a giant bucket of oil. When it was really hot, they would pour it down on the invaders. But look! A bunch of new men on horseback were coming to join the attack. Jared couldn't just watch any longer. He had to join the fight!

DRAW the battle at the castle here:

So you're reading this great story and *wham!* You hit a word you don't know. Do you give up and stop reading? No! You figure out what the word means from the CONTEXT—that means how the word is used. Check it out!

READ this paragraph:

> When I had walked a block from home, it began to rain—hard. I decided to go back and get my geziblet. Back on the street, I opened the geziblet over my head and hurried to the comic book store.

Did you catch the made-up word?

Context Questions:

1. Is a *geziblet* a noun (object), a verb (action), or an adjective (description)? _____

2. When do you need a *geziblet*? _____

3. What do you do with a *geziblet*? _____

4. What's the real word for *geziblet*? _____

See how you used CONTEXT clues to figure it out? If you can figure out a made-up word, you can figure out real words too!

✓ Check It!

Page 277

1. noun
2. when it's raining
3. keep the rain off
4. umbrella

Page 278

What's the Word?

1. verb
2. Percy
3. ask his parents for a dog
4. to pester or bug someone to do something

1. adjective
2. a hill or pit
3. so they can go fast
4. high, vertical, sudden, sharp

Pages 279-280

What's the Word?

1. b
2. a
3. c
4. a
5. get in the way, prevent, or block someone from doing something

Pages 281-282

What's the Word?

1. c
2. b
3. a
4. b
5. dull, inactive, or lazy

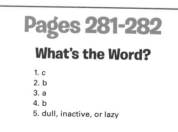

What's the Word?

READ each paragraph, and then FILL IN the blanks by answering the questions.

Percy really wanted a dog. Every day, he asked his parents to let him get one. But his dad was allergic to dogs. There's no way his parents would ever say yes. But Percy asked anyway—every day! Finally, his mother lost her temper. "Percy," she said, "we are never getting a dog, no matter how much you badger us. So you might as well stop asking."

1. Is *badger* being used as a noun, verb, or adjective? _____

2. Who was doing the badgering? _____

3. What did Percy do every day? _____

4. What does the word *badger* mean here? _____

_____

There are lots of different kinds of skateboard parks. But whether they have wooden ramps that tower above the ground, or deep pool-like holes, all skate parks have to give skaters a steep hill or pit so they can get up enough speed to do tricks.

1. Is *steep* being used as a noun, verb, or adjective? _____

2. What does *steep* describe? _____

3. Why do skateboarders need something *steep*? _____

_____

4. What does the word *steep* mean here? _____

_____

What's the Word?

Before you read the story, answer this question: What do you think the word *hinder* means? (It's okay to guess!)

Now READ this paragraph and see if you change your mind.

> Grasshoppers were everywhere! They squashed under our feet in our log cabin. Worst of all, they were eating every bit of grass on the prairie, including our crops! Ma and Pa and Bertie and I rushed out to try and stop them. Ma couldn't run as fast as us because her long skirts hindered her from running. They dragged on the ground and caught on the bushes. Finally, she tied her skirts around her waist, and ran along much faster. But it was too late. The crops were gone.

1. How is *hinder* being used here?

   a. It's a noun.

   b. It's a verb.

   c. It's an adjective.

2. What was hindering Ma?

   a. Her skirts

   b. The grasshoppers

   c. Bertie

READ each context question, and CHECK the correct answer.

3. What was Ma trying to do?

    a. Climb a tree

    b. Read a book

    c. Run fast

4. What were Ma's skirts doing?

    a. Dragging and slowing her down

    b. Pulling her along faster

    c. Lifting her off her feet

5. Now what do you think *hinder* means? _____

_____

_____

What's the Word?

What do you think the word *listless* means? (It's okay to guess!)

_____

_____

Now READ this paragraph and see if you change your mind.

> If you think your pet is sick, there are two things to check before calling the vet. Is your pet eating? If your pet leaves a lot of food in his bowl, that's a bad sign. Is your pet active? If your pet becomes listless and won't play or be friendly, that's also a sign of illness. Pets need a lot of sleep, but too much sleep can be a bad thing!

1. How is *listless* being used here?

   a. It's a noun.

   b. It's a verb.

   c. It's an adjective.

2. What does a listless pet *not* do?

   a. Hide under the bed

   b. Play or be friendly

   c. Sleep or dream

READ each context question, and CHECK the correct answer.

3. What does a listless pet do?

    a. Sleep a lot

    b. Eat a lot

    c. Play a lot

4. Is a listless pet hungry?

    a. Yes

    b. No

5. Now what do you think *listless* means? _____

_____

_____

What's the Word?

What do you think the word *cutlass* means? (It's okay to guess!)

_____

_____

Now READ this paragraph and see if you change your mind.

> Traveling with a princess is a pain. She rides in her fancy coach, with guards on horseback all around her. Guards like me get wet in the rain, and cold in the wind, while she stays snug and warm. In case of attack, each guard must carry a long sword as well as a shorter, curved cutlass. The long sword is good for fighting a battle on horseback. But if a guard loses his horse and needs to fight another man on the ground, the cutlass works better. Hopefully, we won't need either on this trip!

1. How is *cutlass* being used here?

   a. It's a noun.

   b. It's a verb.

   c. It's an adjective.

2. Who carries a *cutlass*?

   a. The princess

   b. The horses

   c. The guards

READ each context question, and CHECK the correct answer.

3. How is the *cutlass* described?

   a. Long and straight

   b. Short and curved

   c. Snug and warm

4. When do you use a *cutlass*?

   a. In battle

   b. When it's dark

   c. When it's cold out

5. Now what do you think *cutlass* means? _____

   _____

   _____

A good story is about a main character (like Cinderella) with a problem (her stepmother won't let her go to the ball). The fun part is how the character solves the problem (hello, Fairy Godmother!). If you start to get lost in a story, look for the problem! Check out this story!

Slippy the Snowkid

The boys on the block made a kid out of snow. They called him Slippy!

Slippy the Snowkid was really cool. He made the best ice forts.

One day it started to get hot. Oh no! Slippy was getting slushy.

The boys brought Slippy to the ice rink! Now Slippy could stay cool.

1. Who's the main character of the story? _____

2. What's the main character's problem? _____

_____

3. How is the problem solved? _____

_____

 Check It!

Page 289

What's the Problem?

1. Olive
2. She wants to dress like a fairy for the picnic, but her mother says she'll be too cold.
3. She creates a "Fairy Firefighter" costume that's warmer than a regular fairy costume. And she wins a prize!

Page 290

What's the Problem?

1. Micah
2. His friend's shoplifting ruins his favorite day.
3. He decides to drop his friend and make a new one.

Page 291

What's the Problem?

1. The SuperSpies M, Q, and K9
2. They need to stop Doc Rotten and his gang from robbing the banks, but the robbers are invisible.
3. SuperSpy Q and Superspy M throw paint on the robbers so they can see them and capture them.

Page 292

What's the Problem?

1. Sanjay
2. Sanjay's two best friends don't get along.
3. Sanjay loses his pet rabbit.
4. Sanjay calls his friends and asks them to get along just while they're hunting for Attila. After that, they find out that being friends is easy!

What's the Problem?

Cowgirl in the City

Tessa wants to be a cowgirl. But she lives in the big city!

She lassos her teddy bear and puts a saddle on a chair.

Finally, the answer!

Cowgirl Tessa on the ranch!

1. Who's the main character of the story? _____

2. What's the main character's problem? _____

_____

3. How is the problem solved? _____

_____

_____

What's the Problem?

The Birthday Bind

Donnell woke up with a gasp. He completely forgot it was Mom's birthday!

He tiptoed out of the house before breakfast. He needed a gift, *fast*!

Donnell didn't have money for candy or a card or flowers.

So Donnell gave Mom a special gift. He did everything she asked all day. She loved it!

1. Who's the main character of the story? _____

2. What's the main character's problem? _____

_____

3. How is the problem solved? _____

_____

_____

What's the Problem?

Jack and the Beanstalk

Jack's mother sent him out to sell their cow.
"Make sure you get lots of money for it!" she said.

But Jack didn't get money. Instead, he traded the cow
for some magic beans.

"We need *money*, not magic beans!" his mother yelled. She pulled Jack's ear
and sent him outside without any supper.

Jack decided to plant the beans. Maybe they were magic, maybe not. But
something should grow, right? Then he slept outside because he knew his
mother was still mad.

When he woke up, Jack was high above the ground! He was lying on a giant leaf
that came out of a giant stalk. It was a beanstalk!

Jack climbed up the beanstalk, just to see how high it went. At the top, he found
a magic land in the clouds. He also found a big bag of gold coins!

"Hey mom!" Jack said, coming back into the house. "Here's that money you
needed." And he dumped the bag of coins on the floor.

That's the last time Jack's mother ever pulled his ear!

1. Main character: _____

2. Problem: _____

_____

3. Solution: _____

_____

_____

_____

What's the Problem?

HINT: Sometimes the problem can be a decision that the main character has to make.

Olive's town was having a big dress-up picnic. She wanted to wear her fairy costume, but her mother said no. "The party's outside and it's too cold," she said.

"I'll wear tights," Olive said. "And a cape over my sparkly pink tank top."

"Pants," said her mother. "Pants and a sweater."

"Fairies don't wear sweaters and pants!" yelled Olive.

"So be a firefighter," said her mother. "Firefighter are warmer than fairies."

Olive stomped up to her room. Her fairy wings were hanging in her closet next to her firefighter outfit. "Hmmmmm," she said.

At the party, they gave a prize to the best costume. "This year's winner is Olive!" said the man in charge. "The Firefighter Fairy!"

Everybody clapped. Olive was wearing fairy wings over her firefighter's jacket, and a crown instead of a helmet. Her firefighter boots were painted with sparkly pink paint.

"How does a fairy fight fires?" asked Missy, who was mean.

Olive rolled her eyes. "Duh!" she said. "I use my magic wand!"

1. Main character: _____

2. Problem: _____

_____

3. Solution: _____

_____

_____

What's the Problem?

Super Saturday

Every Saturday, Micah bought candy and comics and then hit the big skate park. It was his favorite day. One week he thought it would be cool if his friend Tony joined him. Wrong!

See, Tony took some candy, but he didn't pay for it. Then he put two comics in his bag and walked out of the store. When they got to the skate park, Tony was all smiles, but Micah felt sick.

"What's the matter?" asked Tony. "Want some candy?"

"You stole that candy," said Micah, "and some comics."

"Yeah, so?" Tony frowned. "Are you gonna tell on me? Are you a tattletale?"

Micah didn't know what to say. His Saturday was ruined.

The next Saturday, Micah grabbed his skateboard and rolled down the street. When he saw Tony at the corner, he flew straight past him. He bought his candy and comics like usual. When he got to the skate park, Tony was there. But Micah ignored him. He wasn't going to let some dishonest kid ruin his Saturday again. Sheila was skating at the park too, and she was really cool. Maybe she could be Micah's new Saturday friend.

1. Main character: _____

2. Problem: _____

_____

3. Solution: _____

_____

_____

_____

What's the Problem?

HINT: Sometimes the problem can be a decision that the main character has to make.

Doc Rotten Strikes Again

Back at Grizzly Mountain, SuperSpy X was giving his team another mission. "Doc Rotten has made an Invisible Ray. He's going to sneak into the Big Swiss Bank and steal all the money."

So SuperSpy Q, his big sister M, and their dog K9 flew to the Big Swiss Bank. They saw big bags of money floating out the front door!

"It's Doc Rotten and his evil gang!" cried M. "They're all invisible!"

How do you stop robbers you can't see? When the SuperSpies tried to shoot them with their StingRays, they missed. Even K9's superdog nose was confused.

"Ha ha ha!" laughed Doc Rotten. "You'll never catch us."

Then Q had an idea. He ran down the street and bought two cans of black paint from the hardware store. "Come on, Sis!" he cried, handing a can to M. "Throw paint toward the money bags."

When the paint landed on the criminals, the SuperSpies could see them. K9 growled, backing them into a corner, while M and Q wrapped them in SpyNets.

Q called X on his wrist phone. "We caught Doc Rotten," he said. "Mission accomplished!"

1. Main character: _____

2. Problem: _____

3. Solution: _____

What's the Problem?

HINT: You can have more than one problem in a story too.

Rabbit Hunt

Sanjay had two best friends, Marcus and Cherryl. Too bad they hated each other. Sanjay could never hang out with both of his best buds at the same time.

One day on the way to the vet's office, Sanjay's rabbit, Attila, got out of her carrier and hopped away. Sanjay couldn't find her anywhere!

He needed help. But which friend should he call? Cherryl lived the closest, but Marcus had sharp eyes. Sanjay decided to call them both.

"Okay" he said to them, "please try not to fight while we look for Attila."

Marcus and Cherryl frowned at each other. "Okay," they said grumpily.

They searched for a few hours. Marcus used his great eyesight, and Cherryl told him where to look. Finally they found Attila hiding under a bush in the park.

Sanjay was so happy, he took everybody to Pizza Heaven for a great time!

After that day, Marcus and Cherryl stopped hating each other. They found out that being friends is easy when you do it in threes!

1. Main character: _____

2. Problem 1: _____

_____

3. Problem 2: _____

_____

4. Solution: _____

_____

_____

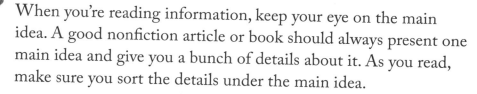

When you're reading information, keep your eye on the main idea. A good nonfiction article or book should always present one main idea and give you a bunch of details about it. As you read, make sure you sort the details under the main idea.

Try it out! SORT these details under the right main idea. FILL IN the blanks with the details.

hooves	cleats	goalie	notes	mane
penalty	tempo	gallop	instruments	

1. Soccer

_____

_____

_____

2. Music

_____

_____

_____

3. Horses

_____

_____

_____

When you stop and think about what you're reading, remember the main idea, and sort those details!

✔ **Check It!**

Page 293

1. cleats
   goalie
   penalty

2. notes
   instruments
   tempo

3. hooves
   mane
   gallop

Page 294

Main idea: Crazy Collections

Details
1. mousetraps
2. refrigerator magnets
3. town signs
4. potato chip bags
5. belly button lint

Page 295

Main idea: Ways to Travel around the World

Details
1. hot air balloon
2. sailboat
3. bicycle
4. airplane
5. satellite

Page 296

Main idea: Eating Contest Foods

Details
1. pies
2. hot dogs
3. lobster
4. jalapeño
5. peppers
6. chicken
7. wings
8. pancakes
9. matzo
10. balls
11. shrimp
12. pizza

Check It!

Page 298

Main idea 1: Winter X Games Events
Details 1. skiing
2. snowboarding
3. snowmobiling

Main idea 2: Summer X Games Events
Details 1. skateboarding
2. BMX bike racing
3. motocross
4. surfing
5. rallying

Page 300

Main Idea 1: Good Guys
Details 1. Seth Bullock
2. Charlie Parks
3. Wyatt Earp
4. Dodge City Peace Commission
5. Pinkerton Agency

Main Idea 2: Bad Guys
Details 1. Billy the Kid
2. Black Bart
3. Butch Cassidy
4. The Wild Bunch Gang
5. Jesse James
6. The James-Younger Gang

READ the paragraph, and FILL IN the main idea and details.

HINT: The details are highlighted.

Crazy Collections

When you think of collections, you probably think about things like trading cards, rocks, or stamps, right? But some people have really whacky collections. Did you know there's a man in Germany with 2,500 mousetraps? How about a woman in Las Vegas who's collected 30,000 refrigerator magnets? There's even a town in Canada with more than 10,000 town signs from all over the world. And the largest collection of potato chip bags belongs to a man in Germany. Then there's the guy in Australia who's been collecting his own belly button lint since 1984! Now that's crazy!

What's the main idea? <u>Crazy collections</u>

List the details:

1. _____

2. _____

3. _____

4. _____

5. _____

READ the paragraph, and FILL IN the main idea and details.

Around the World in 194 days!

There are lots of ways to travel around the world. How much time do you have? In 1999, the first nonstop hot air balloon trip around the world took 19 days, 21 hours, and 55 minutes. Is that too fast for you? Then hop in a sailboat! It'll take you about 60 days to sail around the globe. Still too fast? Try a bike! It took Mark Beaumont 194 days to bike around the world. He rode about 100 miles each day, flew across the oceans, and camped or stayed in hotels at night. If you need to get around the world in a hurry, a nonstop airplane flight around the world only takes about 67 hours. Or hop on a satellite for an even quicker trip. Depending on how high up it flies, a satellite can orbit around the planet in about 100 minutes! Let's go!

What's the main idea? <u>Ways to travel around the world</u>

List the details:

1. _____

2. _____

3. _____

4. _____

5. _____

Main Idea & Details

READ the paragraph, and FILL IN the main idea and details.

Fast Foods

If you're feeling hungry, check out an extreme eating contest. It's more than just pies and hot dogs. At the World Lobster-Eating Championship, someone munched 44 lobsters in 12 minutes! In Nevada, a man ate 247 pickled jalapeño peppers in 8 minutes. Famous hot dog eater Joey Chestnut can also eat 182 chicken wings in 30 minutes (hold the celery!). Other extreme eaters suck down pancakes, matzo balls, shrimp, and pizza. Of course, watching these people stuff their faces might make you lose your appetite!

What's the main idea? _____

_____

List the details:

1. _____

2. _____

3. _____

4. _____

5. _____

6. _____

7. _____

8. _____

9. _____

READ the story, and FILL IN the main idea and details.

HINT: Sometimes there are two main ideas!

Let the X Games Begin!

The X Games is the Olympics of extreme sports. It was started in 1995 by sports channel ESPN. Back then it was called "The Extreme Games." The name was changed to "The X Games" in 1996, and it stuck. Like the Olympics, there's a Winter X Games and a Summer X Games.

The X Games was created to cover sports that are not part of the Olympics. But one of its winter sports, snowboarding, was added to the Olympic list in 1998. And, of course, both events have skiing. But the X Games has an event called "Superpipe Ski" where skiiers zoom through a half-pipe of snow, jumping and doing tricks like skateboarders. The Olympics hasn't added that (yet!). And the Olympics doesn't cover snowmobiling, another Winter X Games event.

The Summer X Games are even more different. In the summer, athletes compete in skateboarding, BMX bike races, motocross, surfing, and rallying (a kind of car racing). Compare that to Olympic events like gymnastics, softball, and table tennis!

Both the Olympics and the X Games have lots of fans. But X Games fans are younger, and as they grow in numbers, the Olympics will probably add more extreme sports to its line-up.

Now, TURN the page and FILL IN the blanks!

FILL IN the blanks with main ideas and details.

Main Idea 1: <u>Winter X Games events</u>

Main Idea 2: <u>Summer X Games events</u>

Details:

1. _____

2. _____

3. _____

Details:

1. _____

2. _____

3. _____

4. _____

5. _____

READ the story, and FILL IN the main idea and details.

Good Guys and Bad Guys

In the Old West, there were good guys and bad guys.

One bad guy, Billy the Kid, was a cattle "rustler" who stole cows and other livestock from people's farms. As for Black Bart, he used to rob the Wells Fargo stagecoaches that brought mail, money, and goods from the east. Black Bart robbed 28 stagecoaches!

On the good side, sheriffs like Seth Bullock kept law and order in wild western towns. And men like Charlie Parks worked hard to protect the mail. Parks started out as a rider on the Pony Express and then became a guard for Wells Fargo. Legend has it that he had more bullet wounds in his body than any other man in California!

Sometimes outlaw gangs would ride into towns and rob the banks. Butch Cassidy had "The Wild Bunch" gang. Jesse James had a gang called "The James-Younger Gang."

But there were good gangs too. The Dodge City Peace Commission, headed by famous sheriff Wyatt Earp, protected the people of their town. And the Pinkerton Agency sent detectives out west to hunt down outlaws like Jesse James and Butch Cassidy.

In the end, the good guys won out. Today people who live in the west know that their homes, towns, and mail are safe and secure!

Now, TURN the page and FILL IN the blanks!

Main Idea & Details

HINT: Sometimes there are two main ideas!

Main Idea 1: _____

_____

Details:

1. _____

2. _____

3. _____

4. _____

5. _____

Main Idea 2: _____

_____

Details:

1. _____

2. _____

3. _____

4. _____

5. _____

6. _____

You've read lots of stories, so you know how they work. A story is a bunch of events that happen in a certain order. If you keep track of these events, you'll know where you are in the story. Let's read one and see.

The Three Big Pigs

Hammy, Jammy, and Sammy were three big pigs. Hammy made his house out of straw. Jammy built his out of sticks. And Sammy constructed a big mansion out of bricks. One day, Wolfie Growl came to town. He liked to eat big pigs, so he went to Hammy's house. He huffed and puffed and blew Hammy's lame straw house down. Then he did the same thing to Jammy's house. But when Wolfie got to Sammy's big mansion, he blew until he was blue, but nothing happened. So Wolfie picked the lock, broke into the house, and ate up all three pigs. Burp!

Now, DRAW a line to match each event with its order in the story.

Order	Event
1. First	a. Hammy, Jammy, and Sammy build their houses.
2. Second	b. Wolfie breaks into Sammy's house and eats all three pigs.
3. Third	c. Wolfie can't blow down Sammy's house.
4. Finally	d. Wolfie Growl blows down Hammy and Jammy's house.

Easy, right? But sometimes the author doesn't tell you the story in the right order. So watch out!

✓ **Check It!**

Page 301

1. a
2. d
3. c
4. b

Page 302

1. c
2. a
3. d
4. b

Page 303

1. c
2. a
3. b
4. d

Page 305

1. h
2. g
3. c
4. d
5. i
6. b

Story Plan

✓ **Check It!**

Page 307

3
4
1
6
5
2

Page 308

3
1
4
6
5
2

READ the story.

Rain Delay

The Wildcats were winning. Their grand slam homerun in the first inning scored them four points. Then the Kingfishers got three runs in the second inning.

But it was so *hot*! By the sixth inning, sweat was streaming off all the Kingfishers in the outfield. The air was so thick, it was hard to breathe.

Suddenly, a little boy in the stands started to dance. He was Andy Kolchak's little brother.

"Stop!" yelled Andy, waving from the outfield. "*Stop*!"

But it was too late. Rain poured from the sky. The coaches ended the game early.

Andy took off his cap and smacked his brother in the behind. "Couldn't you have waited for us to tie the score before doing your stupid rain dance?"

"I was hot!" yelled his brother, dancing in the rain.

Now, DRAW a line to match each event with its order in the story.

Order

1. First

2. Second

3. Third

4. Finally

Event

a. The Kingfishers get three runs in the second inning.

b. The game ends early and the Wildcats win.

c. The Wildcats score four runs with a grand slam.

d. Andy's little brother does a rain dance.

READ the story.

HINT: Sometimes the author doesn't tell you the story in the right order. So watch out!

What's Justin's Problem?

After the big math test, Justin didn't know what to do. He felt terrible. Maybe he could talk to Mom? But when he went home, she had left for work. Justin lay on his bed. This is a serious problem, he thought.

At the bus stop the next day, Justin walked right up to his best friend, Mack.

"I saw you cheat on the math test yesterday," he said.

Mack looked sick and scared. "Are you going to tell Mr. Sam?" he asked.

Justin shrugged. "I don't know what to do."

The two boys didn't talk on the ride to school. Justin followed Mack off the bus and up the steps. At the doors, Mack turned around.

"Will you come with me?" he asked. "To tell?"

Justin smiled and said, "Of course! That's what best friends are for."

Now, DRAW a line to match each event with its order in the story.

Order

1. First
2. Second
3. Third
4. Finally

Event

a. Justin goes home and thinks about what to do.

b. Justin tells Mack what he saw.

c. Justin sees Mack cheat on the math test.

d. Mack and Justin go to tell the teacher.

READ the story.

Princess Pretty and the Beast

Once upon a time, there was a very ugly prince with a big scaly wart on the end of his nose. This prince also had hairy hands, hairy feet, and a hairy back. He even had sprouts of hair coming out of his ears!

The prince was named Zigfried, but everyone called him "Beast." He walked around looking at the ground and never smiled.

One day there was a carriage crash outside the prince's castle. The servants brought in a young lady who had hurt her head. The doctor said she needed to rest at the castle for two weeks with a cloth wrapped around her eyes.

Those two weeks were the best time Beast had ever had. The young lady was named Princess Pretty. She and Beast spent every day together, talking and laughing.

On the day the doctor returned, Beast ran away to hide. He was afraid that the princess wouldn't like him anymore once she could see.

When the doctor took off the cloth, the princess could see perfectly. She was so happy, she ran all over the castle to tell Beast. She found him in a very dark room.

"Hey Ziggy!" (She called him Ziggy.) "Are you hiding from me?"

"Um, no." Ziggy stepped forward into the light.

"Oh, dear!" the princess cried. "You really need a shave. And something must be done about that awful wart. Tsk-tsk-tsk!"

So Princess Pretty dragged the Beast to the nearest salon and had the barbers pluck his ears and wax his hands and feet. They trimmed his eyebrows and shaved his beard. They even took off his wart! When they were done, the princess gave Beast a kiss.

It worked like magic. Suddenly, Prince Ziggy stood up straight and smiled. He was really very handsome!

Now, DRAW a line to match each event with its order in the story.

HINT: Some of the events didn't happen in the story. Cross those out.

Order

1. First
2. Second
3. Third
4. Fourth
5. Fifth
6. Finally

Event

a. Princess Pretty breaks the fairy's spell.

b. Ziggy smiles and looks handsome.

c. Princess Pretty and Ziggy become friends.

d. The doctor takes off Princess Pretty's bandage.

e. Ziggy kidnaps the Princess from her home.

f. Princess Pretty ran away from the castle.

g. There's a carriage crash outside the castle.

h. An ugly Prince Zigfried never smiled.

i. Princess Pretty takes Ziggy to the salon.

K9 Saves the Day

One day, the SuperSpies were called to a meeting at Grizzly Mountain. Instead of seeing SuperSpy X, they saw a new SuperSpy, who wore a blue mask. He said his code name was D.

"Where's X?" asked SuperSpy Q.

"He's on a secret mission," said SuperSpy D. "So I'm in charge. And I have a special job for SuperSpies M and K9. We need to fly to Paris right away!"

So M and K9 left with SuperSpy D.

"That's weird," said Q. "I usually work with M and K9."

"Maybe the new guy doesn't know you're M's little brother," said SuperSpy T.

"Yeah, maybe you'll get your own missions from now on!" said SuperSpy F.

But Q was worried. He went for a walk around the underground SpyStation. He was passing a closet when he heard a strange knocking sound. He tried to open the door, but it was locked.

"SuperSpies T and F, I need your help!" Q called into his wrist radio.

T and F came running, and together the three spies busted down the door to the closet. Inside they found SuperSpy X tied to a chair with a gag in his mouth so he couldn't call for help!

"X, what happened?" asked Q after they untied the prisoner.

"It's Doc Rotten! He snuck into our secret headquarters and knocked me out."

"He's pretending to be SuperSpy D!" cried T.

"And he's got my sister!" yelled Q.

The SuperSpies had to act fast. They jumped into their SpyShuttles and used their tracking rays to find SuperSpies M and K9.

But when they found the SuperSpies, the action was over. M and K9 had Doc Rotten wrapped in SpyNets, and they were waiting for the police.

"K9 knew D was a fake as soon as she saw him," said M, patting K9 on the head.

"How did she know?" asked Q.

"She could tell by the smell!" said M. "Superdogs make SuperSpies!"

Now, NUMBER the events to show the order in which they happened.

HINT: The events are listed the way they were told to you, not necessarily in the order they happened.

3 SuperSpy D took M and K9 away.

4 Q found X locked in a closet.

1 Doc Rotten snuck into the SpyStation and knocked out X.

6 The SuperSpies found M and K9.

5 M and K9 overpowered Doc Rotten

and tied him up.

2 K9 knew right away that D

was really Doc Rotten.

Story Plan

READ the story.

A Mixed Up Story

My brother can't tell a story to save his life! Check out this note he left me:

Patti: We're at the hospital because the dog ran away. It all started when I left the vacuum cleaner sitting in the middle of the living room. When Jiggers got out, I forgot all about it. Mr. Hashiro rang the bell, and when I opened the door— ZOOM!—Jiggers was off. We tried to chase him, but he's too fast. But then Mom ran to the door and tripped over the vacuum cleaner. She was running because she saw Jiggers coming down the street. She had been looking out the kitchen window, doing dishes. Anyway, it's just a broken ankle. Mom's mad, but she'll be fine. And Jiggers is locked in the basement. I found him sitting on the front steps.

—Kyle

Kyle messed up the order of his story. Can you put it back together? NUMBER the events to show the order in which they happened.

_3_ Kyle and Mr. Hashiro chased after him.

_1_ Kyle was vacuuming when the doorbell rang.

_4_ Meanwhile, Mom was in the kitchen doing dishes when she saw Jiggers coming down the street.

_6_ Kyle found Jiggers sitting on the front steps and locked him in the basement before going with his mom to the hospital.

_5_ She ran through the living room, tripped over the vacuum and broke her ankle.

_2_ Kyle opened the door and Jiggers the dog ran away.